The low point of labor resistance is behind us

The low point of labor resistance is behind us

THE SOCIALIST WORKERS PARTY LOOKS FORWARD

JACK BARNES

MARY-ALICE WATERS

STEVE CLARK

PATHFINDER

NEW YORK LONDON MONTREAL SYDNEY

Edited by Steve Clark and Mary-Alice Waters

ISBN 978-1-60488-145-5
Library of Congress Control Number 2022952458
Manufactured in Canada

First edition, 2023
Second printing, 2023

COVER DESIGN: Toni Gorton

FRONT COVER PHOTOS, CLOCKWISE FROM TOP:

Topeka, Kansas, July 2021: BCTGM Local 218 at Frito-Lay on strike over forced overtime and wages. (*Topeka Frito-Lay Union Members Appreciation Page*)

Brookwood, Alabama, June 2021: Coal miners picket Warrior Met Coal. (*UMWA Journal*)

New York, January 2020: Joanne Kuniansky, Socialist Workers Party candidate for Congress in New Jersey, at rally against attacks on Jews. (*Roy Landersen/Militant*)

BACK COVER PHOTOS, COUNTERCLOCKWISE FROM TOP:

October 2022: Crowds at cemetery in Kurdish region of Iran protest death of Zhina Amini during custody by Tehran's "morality" police.

Toa Baja, Puerto Rico, September 2022: Milagros Rivera, president of Cuba solidarity committee, protesting FBI harassment. (*Courtesy of Wanda I. González*)

Galesburg, Illinois, July 2022: Rail workers and supporters rally during contract battle. (*Courtesy of Jeff Schuhrke*)

PATHFINDER
www.pathfinderpress.com
E-mail: pathfinder@pathfinderpress.com

CONTENTS

PHOTOS AND ILLUSTRATIONS

Preface

BY MARY-ALICE WATERS

The Low Point of Labor Resistance Is Behind Us: The Socialist Workers Party Looks Forward is the product of trade union and broader political work over the last year by SWP members responding to deepening cracks in the world order established by the victors of the inter-imperialist slaughter known in the United States as World War II.

This activity by party members, shoulder to shoulder with other working people and youth, is being carried out amid mounting global conflicts among rival capitalist powers, with explosive ramifications for workers and farmers in the Americas, Europe, the Mideast, Africa, Asia, and Pacific.

Above all, the articles and documents here highlight the opportunities ahead for class-conscious workers, as a decades-long retreat by the working class and trade unions comes to an end. The intensified speedup, longer and longer hours, attacks on job safety, declining real wages, lack of steady employment, and spiraling social and moral blight—conditions produced by the ruling class families in the United States and capitalism's dog-eat-dog social relations—are pressing more and more working people to say, "Enough is enough." Workers have begun using our collective economic power and class solidarity in response.

The material compiled in these pages has been written and prepared for publication by the Editing Commission of the Socialist Workers Party National Committee: Jack Barnes, Steve Clark, Dave Prince, and Mary-Alice Waters. It opens with an article from the *Militant* newsweekly, "published in the interests of working people," as its masthead proudly proclaims. The article reports on the June 9–12, 2022 International Active Workers Conference organized by the SWP, with some 350 participants from eleven countries.

The contents include two SWP National Committee policy statements.

One, in defense of Ukraine's independence and sovereignty, was released March 3, 2022, in the opening days of Moscow's invasion, launched with the avowed aim of erasing the very existence of its neighbor.

The other was issued on October 11, 2022, in the wake of Hurricane Ian's devastating path across western Cuba. Consistent with the SWP's history the statement, like many before it, demands an immediate end to the US government's six-decades long murderous attempt to crush Cuban working people for their audacity in making a socialist revolution in what Washington considers its own backyard.

The heart of the book, from which the title is taken, is the political resolution adopted December 12, 2022, by the 49th Constitutional Convention of the Socialist Workers Party. It sets forth the course of action that has guided the party's work and will continue to do so—the course necessary today to forge mass proletarian parties and an international communist movement able to lead the struggle to end capitalist rule.

As the opening lines of the SWP Constitution state, the purpose of the party is to advance the education and organization of the working class "in order to establish a workers and farmers government which will abolish capitalism in the United States and join in the worldwide struggle for socialism."

◆

The resolution is written in the form of twenty-seven numbered sections, yet none of the questions engaged here stand alone. They can be understood only as part of the line of march of the working class to state power, the political line of the resolution as a whole.

Among the questions addressed are:

• Why the fight to prevent erosion by the capitalist government—both in Washington, as well as in the fifty states—of freedoms protected by the US Constitution is central to the US class struggle today. Freedom from government *intervention* and constraints on worship, on speech, on the press, on due process, on a trial by a jury of one's peers (not forced confessions in the form of "plea bargains"), and more. This includes opposing the US rulers' expanding use of Washington's political police, the FBI above all.

• Why the tenacious maintenance of the US Supreme Court and judiciary as courts of *written law,* not de facto legislative bodies, is essential to defense of the liberties of working people under the Constitution.

• Why socialist revolution is impossible without a fight to build the trade unions and transform them into independent instruments of class struggle, wielded by class-conscious, battle-tested members.

• Why the working class needs a labor party based on the unions, a labor party that could present a complete break from the illusion that the parties or candidates of the imperialist rulers can represent us. A party that speaks and acts in the interests of the working class and oppressed as a whole. A party that rejects demagogic appeals to the politics of resentment, used by both the capitalist Democratic and Republican parties to appeal to and pit against each other insecure layers of the middle class and sections of the toilers.

• Why there is no road to African American liberation— no end to racist discrimination and the legacy of centuries of slavery and then Jim Crow terror and oppression—separate and apart from the working-class course toward a victorious socialist revolution.

• Why the fight against Jew-hatred, on the rise across the world today, must be integral to the program and strategy of the revolutionary workers movement, and of all organizations of the exploited and oppressed.

• Why the fight for women's emancipation is inextricably intertwined with addressing the capitalist-caused crises of joblessness and inflation; the lack of affordable medical care, childcare, and housing; as well as drug addiction and domestic violence—all of which bear down on the families of working people, and on women especially. Why there should be no federal, state, or municipal laws restricting the safe medical availability of abortions.

• Why a revolutionary party must be proletarian in composition as well as program and leadership.

• Why the positions reaffirmed by SWP convention delegates trace their continuity from the founders in 1847 of the modern revolutionary workers movement, Karl Marx and Frederick Engels, and the world's first communist party they led. To the opening years of the first victorious socialist revolution, the Bolshevik Revolution of 1917 under the leadership of V.I. Lenin. To the example of Cuba's socialist revolution under the leadership of Fidel Castro and the leading cadres of the Rebel Army. And to the SWP's class-struggle experience from the founding of the first communist party in the US in 1919 down to today.

• Why the Transitional Program, the 1938 founding resolution of the Socialist Workers Party and of our world movement, remains at the center of our program to this day.

◆

Asserting that "the low point of labor resistance is behind us" is not a prediction about coming struggles. Nor is it a promise about when or where new and more powerful class battles will break out. Instead, that assessment is based on the increased confidence and combativity, as well as the anger demonstrated by working people confronting very different conditions around the world.

We've seen it during the post-COVID economic "recovery" with strikes, organizing efforts, and other union fights in the United States by bakery workers, rail freight workers, coal miners, and other unionists, as well as by others organizing to establish unions where they work.

We've seen it in fights by public education workers and truckers in Canada, by rail workers and nurses in the United Kingdom, and by workers and unionists from Australia, South Korea, and Russia to Israel, South Africa, and Puerto Rico.

We've seen it in the mass revolt in China against the brutal, anti-working-class COVID policies of the Stalinist regime in Beijing.

In the hundreds of thousands of youth and working people who've taken to the streets across Iran in response to the death of Zhina Amini at the hands of the hated "morality" police.

In the determination of the toilers of Ukraine to roll back Moscow's attempt to wipe them off the map.

In the steadfastness of Cuban working people in defending their socialist revolution in face of the mounting human and material hardships inflicted by Washington's brutal, decades-long economic, trade, financial, and diplomatic drive to crush the revolution.

◆

The Low Point of Labor Resistance Is Behind Us: The Socialist Workers Party Looks Forward is a companion to two other Pathfinder books, one published in late 2021, the other forthcoming in 2023. Both develop central aspects of the SWP's program and activity addressed here in the party's 2022 convention resolution.

Labor, Nature, and the Evolution of Humanity: The Long View of History is a defense of Marxism—a defense of the proletarian line of march toward power, historical materialism, and basic physical and biological science—against what the resolution calls the "anti-working-class race-baiting, wokery, and 'cancel culture' on the bourgeois and petty bourgeois left."

The second book, coming later this year, brings back into print the 1960 booklet *Too Many Babies? The Myth of the Population Explosion* by SWP leader Joseph Hansen, along with Lenin's writings on the working-class road to women's emancipation. The Bolshevik leader intransigently condemns capitalist population control notions, pointing to their "completely reactionary nature and ugliness."

"Anti-working-class 'overpopulation' demagogy," the SWP resolution notes, "is still rife among bourgeois and middle-class 'environmentalists,' climate doomsayers, scientists, and organizations claiming to champion women's rights. This includes 'counseling' working-class women and their spouses, often misrepresented as family planning, to bring fewer children into the world."

As the document explains, Lenin contrasted "such an outlook to that of 'the class-conscious worker,' who is confident in 'the working-class movement and its aims' and who says instead: 'We are already laying the foundation of a new edifice and our children will complete its construction'—and their children, and their children!"

Together, these three books underline the more and more pressing reality that the working-class forces capable of forging that "new edifice" are being born and will be born in the class battles of the world-in-becoming.

The proletarian internationalist party-building course presented in these pages is the only one that can lead to victory. It's the only one worth fighting for. The future of humanity is in the balance.

January 2, 2023

Taking the Socialist Workers Party's program to the toilers

STEVE CLARK AND TERRY EVANS

"WE HAVE AN UNUSUAL OPPORTUNITY this year to go straight out of this conference into campaigning and other activity focused on the central political and programmatic questions we're discussing and clarifying here," said Jack Barnes, national secretary of the Socialist Workers Party. He was speaking June 11 to some 350 people taking part in the SWP-sponsored International Active Workers Conference at Wittenberg University in Springfield, Ohio.

This year's annual gathering, the largest since 2009, drew attendance from eleven countries, including members and supporters from the SWP's sister Communist Leagues in Canada, the United Kingdom, New Zealand, and Australia, as well as participants from France, Greece, Iran, Iceland, Norway, and Sweden. The end of COVID-related lockdowns and travel restrictions in most parts of the world made it possible for the first time in three years to hold a truly international gathering, making it stronger politically.

This article appeared in the July 4, 2022, issue of the *Militant*, a socialist newsweekly published in the interests of working people.

"We have an unusual opportunity to go straight out of this conference into campaigning and other activity focused on the central programmatic questions we're discussing." —*Jack Barnes*

Top: April 2022. California SWP candidates Ellie García and Joel Britton visit farmer near Fresno to discuss water access and other challenges facing small producers and the need to forge a worker-farmer alliance.

CAROLE LESNICK/MILITANT

LAURA ANDERSON/MILITANT

Middle: October 2022. Rachele Fruit, left, SWP candidate for governor of Florida, talks with Duchelande St. Fleur, a cook, and her husband, Peter Carmant, a trucker, about the SWP program on their doorstep in North Miami.

Bottom: Princeville, Quebec, June 2022. Katy LeRougetel (right), Communist League candidate in Quebec provincial election, speaks with Kiève Parisée in town northeast of Montreal. Parisée and her husband told her they had just been laid off.

ANNETTE KOURI/MILITANT

"Take the SWP program to the toilers! Extend the reach of the party's candidates, press, and books. Join the Socialist Workers Party!"—that was the banner at the front of the auditorium. At a rally on the closing night, communist workers talked about highlights of the spring's successful propaganda campaigns and the party's trade union and other activity, as well as plans for continued campaigning this summer and fall.

These next steps include winning hundreds of subscription renewals from the nearly 1,700 new readers of the *Militant;* getting books by party leaders and other revolutionists into the hands of working people and youth; and using communist election campaigns and candidates to explain the party's program. There will be a special July effort to win a federal ballot spot in Pennsylvania—for the first time in many years—for SWP candidate for US Congress in Philadelphia, Chris Hoeppner.

Speakers at the closing event also described organizing solidarity with hard-fought strikes by workers and their unions.

The SWP will hold a December convention, Barnes said. Based on discussion by the membership of material prepared by the party leadership, branches will choose delegates who will debate and decide the party's course and next steps, and elect a National Committee.

Capitalist crisis, workers' response

Conference proceedings were organized around plenary reports on today's accelerating capitalist economic, social, and moral crises; sharpening conflicts among imperialist ruling classes and other powers; and the resulting receptivity among working people to the perspectives of the SWP and communist organizations in other countries.

The conference political report by Jack Barnes pointed to accelerating inflation, a developing sharp downturn in production and trade, and the consequences for the living and job conditions of workers and our families. Working people face the spread of deadly drugs, alcoholism, and gambling addiction (the latter more and more directly promoted by the ruling class), as well as rising rates of mental illness, suicide, and crime.

Amid these conditions, Barnes said, the working class more than ever has a stake in defending the freedoms and protections codified in the US Constitution, which provide political space we need to organize and fight. These rights are under assault by the bosses' government and political parties, with middle-class "progressives" more and more often in the forefront of pressing to restrict rights and silence their critics.

The presentation by SWP National Committee member Mary-Alice Waters—"The Family and Women's Emancipation: What Two Socialist Revolutions and Our Own Class-Struggle Experience Have Taught Us"—politically armed conference participants to more effectively bring a working-class voice into the raging debate opened earlier this year over the leaked US Supreme Court draft that would overturn the 1973 *Roe v. Wade* abortion decision. [The court issued its decision in the case of *Dobbs v. Jackson Women's Health Organization* on June 24, 2022.]

There was a presentation on "Moscow's War against Ukraine Opens New Stage in Crisis of Imperialist World Order" by *Militant* editor John Studer, as well as a report on the party's work in the unions and labor movement by SWP trade union director Mary Martin.

The presentations were complemented by two question and discussion sessions on the presentations, as well as four classes: "Independent Working-Class Politics vs. Class Collaboration: Lessons from the Struggle for Black Liberation"; "The SWP and Exploited Farmers: An Ally in the Fight for Working-Class Power"; "Lenin, the Bund, and Forging the Bolshevik Party"; and "In Defense of Marxism: The Party's Proletarian Orientation and Our Communist Program."

More than a dozen displays illustrating conference themes lined one side of the auditorium, attracting participants before and after each session.

Table after table of books welcomed everyone as they entered the hall, with 620 bought overall. Top sellers were more than fifty copies of various issues of *New International* magazine featuring articles exploring the roots of today's breakdowns and wars, as well as *The Emancipation of Women* by V.I. Lenin; the 1957 SWP resolution *The Class Struggle Road to Negro Equality*; *Marxism and the Working Farmer*; and the latest Pathfinder Press title, *Labor, Nature, and the Evolution of Humanity*.

Lively mealtime discussions and evening social activities capped the days.

Crises and war

We live in a world marked by sharp shifts in the "imperialist order" imposed by the victors of World War II, said Barnes. These conflicts have been building for years and have been considerably accelerated by Moscow's war against the people of Ukraine.

Cutthroat competition for profits tears at the patchwork of stronger versus weaker capitalist states in the so-called European Union, with utter disregard for working people's life and limb. Currency and trade wars are sharpening, with their transformation into shooting wars on the horizon. The expansionist-minded, Stalinist-molded regime in Beijing poses stepped-up challenges to Washington in Asia, the Pacific, and elsewhere.

The central target of the propertied US rulers is working people, who are not only scorned as "deplorables" but increasingly *feared* by "enlightened" social layers.

Capitalism's economic stresses on our families are weighing on birth rates and bringing increasing pressures on families caring for elderly parents and other relatives.

The class struggle is marked by sharp shifts in today's "world order," accelerated by Moscow's war against Ukraine, by trade wars, and by challenges posed to US imperialism by the expansionist regime in Beijing.

The central target of the propertied rulers and their comfortable middle-class water carriers is working people. During the 2016 presidential campaign, Hillary Clinton scorned the vast majority of them as "deplorables," not only deeply despised but increasingly *feared* by self-proclaimed "enlightened" social layers. It is this fear that's driving the crisis and factionalism shaking the rulers' twin Democratic and Republican Parties and other US political, state, educational, and cultural institutions.

But for the SWP, Barnes said, it is exactly the vast majority of "deplorables"—of all backgrounds, regions, and skin colors, both sexes, city and country—"who we are trying to win. That's who we're trying to educate, to raise class consciousness. That's who we're learning from."

This fear and disdain for the working class among liberals and the radical left explains much of their panic, real or hyped, over the leaked Supreme Court draft. These middle class "social justice warriors" insist that workers and other small producers—not the capitalist system of exploitation and oppression—are the root of all prejudice and reaction. They peddle the utterly false notion that reversing *Roe v. Wade* opens a "slippery slope" that threatens every hard-fought gain for the oppressed over the past half century.

Barnes pointed to the fact that polls show public support today for the right of two people of the same sex to marry has grown to over 70 percent of the population. Support for marriage rights of two individuals regardless of race is even higher, at 94 percent.

There's broad support for "Miranda rights," which place restraints on how cops can entrap you. There's no substantial challenge to access to contraception, or motion toward restoring "sodomy laws" victimizing gays.

These rights conquered in past struggles are today recognized and supported by hundreds of millions. They won't be easily taken away, Barnes said, nor are significant forces organizing to do so.

These major shifts in attitudes extend to growing interest in trade unions, Barnes said. A recent poll shows that more people look favorably on trade unions today than at any time in many decades.

Nothing similar can be said about attitudes toward abortion since 1973, when *Roe v. Wade* was handed down. That ruling undermined the fight for women's rights. The subsequent half century has left popular opinion on a woman's access to safe, legal abortion more class-divided and polarized than ever before. It is the professional and better-off middle classes who are hysterical over *Roe v. Wade*, not working people in their big majority.

Barnes noted that the US Constitution explicitly enumerates rights that government bodies cannot take away, as well as other limitations and restrictions on the powers of the state, including the federal structure of national and state governments. The Constitution was ratified some 230 years ago by the ruling families to buffer factional divisions among themselves. But its hard-fought-for amendments better serve the needs of workers to organize and fight independently of our exploiters and oppressors than do the laundry lists of "granted" rights that mark constitutions of France, Canada, South Africa, and other "enlightened" regimes.

Better for working people to have protections *against* the bosses' state, than "rights" (conditionally) "given" to us *by that state*.

The US rulers, Barnes said, seek to mask the social ills bred by the profit system by legitimizing and promoting these evils as newly found "freedoms" for working people. He gave the example of today's New York City subway ads, which claim that using drugs the "right way" can be "empowering." And New York Mayor Eric Adams's celebration of the legalization of marijuana in the state as a big money-maker and investment attraction for the city fathers.

Barnes pointed out that the late US Senator from New York—Daniel Patrick Moynihan, a Democratic Party politician, member of both the Lyndon Johnson and Richard Nixon administrations, and Social Democratic–leaning

"Woke progressives" peddle the lie that workers are the root of prejudice and reaction, not the capitalist system of exploitation and oppression.

Top: Leesburg, Virginia, June 2021. Parents protest school programs that divide students by race and teach that children with white skin are racist by birth.

ANDREW CABALLERO-REYNOLDS/AFP

KEVIN BANATTE

Middle: January 2017 Women's March on Washington. Its middle-class organizers blamed "deplorable" white workers for women's second-class status.

GRACIE POZO CHRISTIE

Bottom: Hollywood, Florida, pregnancy center defaced in May 2022 by thugs known as "Jane's Revenge," who claim to act in the interests of women's rights. Violent attacks not only on "right-to-life" clinics but also Catholic churches and other religious sites have surged following Supreme Court actions annulling *Roe v. Wade* decision.

The US rulers seek to mask social crises by "normalizing" and "legalizing" them. Drug addiction is declared to be benign "recreation" despite the soaring deaths.

"Don't be ashamed you are using, be empowered that you are using safely."

FLORENCE, Manhattan

What is Fentanyl?

Fentanyl is a powerful opioid that can be found in heroin, cocaine, crack, methamphetamine, ketamine, and pressed pills.

Why is it Dangerous?

Fentanyl increases the risk of overdose especially among people who do not regularly use opioids.

Prevent overdose:

- Avoid using alone and take turns
- Start with a small dose and go slowly
- Have naloxone on hand
- Avoid mixing drugs
- Test your drugs using fentanyl test strips

LET'S PREVENT OVERDOSE. KEEP YOURSELF AND YOUR COMMUNITY SAFE.

TO FIND SUPPORT, INCLUDING NALOXONE OR TREATMENT. CALL 1-888-NYC-WELL OR TEXT "WELL" TO 65173.

NYC Health

Eric L. Adams
Mayor
Ashwin Vasan, MD, PhD
Commissioner

NEW YORK CITY DEPARTMENT OF HEALTH

Above: Ad on New York subways urges riders to use drugs "safely." Mayor Eric Adams boasts city will reap $1.25 billion in taxes from legalized marijuana. "The cannabis industry can be a major boon to our economic recovery," he says.

advocate of capitalism—coined an accurate term for this phenomenon: *"Defining deviancy down."* It describes, Moynihan said, how some officials and public figures, in face of the growing social ills, "benefit from redefining the problem as essentially normal."

SWP branches, Barnes said, will be organizing to read and discuss this article, along with others by Moynihan that describe how the family under contemporary conditions is the only place working people can turn for help in face of joblessness, social inequality, and other crises imposed on us.

The future for working people in the US, Barnes emphasized, remains intertwined with Cuba's socialist revolution, which marked the renewal of communist leadership in the Americas and beyond. The Cuban toilers' conquest of state power, under the political leadership of Fidel Castro and of the Rebel Army, set a powerful example for working people in the US of what we are capable of accomplishing and why we are building a revolutionary workers party in this country.

Defend Ukraine's independence!

"No political organization is better prepared to explain the stakes for working people in reversing Moscow's invasion of Ukraine than the Socialist Workers Party," *Militant* editor and SWP National Committee member John Studer said in his conference report. Studer led three reporting teams to Ukraine after the working-class and popular Maidan uprising of 2014 overthrew the Moscow-backed regime. They reported on the conditions facing workers and their fight for national independence.

Since Moscow's invasion early this year, party members have campaigned with an SWP National Committee statement that explains that the party is mobilizing its candidates to use the 2022 election campaign "to get out the truth and present an independent foreign policy" that "starts from the interests of the toilers at home and internationally." The statement gives unconditional support to the fight for Ukrainian independence and sovereignty and demands an immediate end to Moscow's military operations and occupation.

The SWP demands a halt to all of Washington's economic, banking, and trade sanctions against Russia, whose devastation falls overwhelmingly on working people in Russia, undercutting solidarity between workers and soldiers in the two countries. The statement also demands Washington withdraw *all* its nuclear weapons and armed forces from Europe.

Studer explained that the support for national self-determination in Ukraine is rooted in the SWP's political continuity with communist leader V.I. Lenin, who in October 1917 led working people in Russia, under the leadership of the Bolshevik party, in overturning rule by the capitalists and landlords and bringing to power a workers and peasants republic. That revolutionary government not only launched the fight against exploitation of the working class and peasantry, but also replaced the tsarist empire's subjugation of oppressed nations and peoples with a *voluntary union*—the Union of Soviet Socialist Republics.

Lenin's proletarian internationalist course was turned into the program of the Communist International founded in 1919, with the aim of building working-class parties the world over organizing to emulate the Bolsheviks' revolutionary example. Only with the counterrevolutionary reversal of these policies in the late 1920s by Joseph Stalin, and the petty-bourgeois social layer on whose behalf he spoke and acted, was the unconditional right to self-determination of oppressed nations snuffed out in the Soviet Union.

SWP members have gotten the *Militant*—the only working-class source of news on the Ukraine war and its consequences—into the hands of coworkers on the job, on their doorsteps, at strike picket lines, as well as to working farmers.

Studer described the interest in issues of *New International* magazine by participants at recent book fairs in Havana, Tehran, Los Angeles and elsewhere in the US. These issues explain the root causes of wars in the imperialist epoch, and how the US rulers emerged from World War II atop the imperialist pecking order.

But the so-called American Century abruptly came to an end before it had barely begun, with the defeat of Washington's goals in the Korean and Vietnam wars as milestones, matched by a relative erosion of its commanding economic dominance as well.

With the coming apart of the Soviet Union at the opening of the 1990s—what Cuban communist leader Fidel Castro called "the fall of the meringue"—the US imperialist rulers had *lost* the Cold War not won it, as many of its political, military, and academic apologists initially trumpeted. This fact has been registered in the trail of stalemated or lost wars waged by Washington in Iraq, Libya, Afghanistan, and elsewhere—and the deaths and destruction left in the wake of these assaults.

This outcome for US imperialism, however, has not been accompanied by the rise of any new capitalist power to replace it, Studer said. The impossibility of a historic surrogate for the world's final empire was aptly put some thirty-five years ago in the SWP resolution, "What the 1987

Stock Market Crash Foretold," published in *New International* no. 10. "Despite intensifying competition for profits on the world market," it says, "the rival national ruling classes are chained together in their decline, with the US capitalist rulers at their head."

Before the calamitous events imperialism is marching us toward, the working class will have our chance to win state power. A victorious outcome isn't inevitable. *That depends on us.*

Today, accelerated by Moscow's invasion, rival capitalist powers are rushing to prepare for future conflicts. The direction of capitalist development can be seen more clearly by working people—a march toward fascism and world war, horrifically confirmed in the last century.

"The future of humanity depends on the independent political organization of the world's toilers," Studer said. "It is in our hands to take war-making powers out of the hands of the exploiters, to prevent the calamities that imperialism is marching, and stumbling, toward.

"But before the culmination of such calamitous events, the working class here will have our chance—*if* we can forge a mass revolutionary proletarian party able to mobilize and lead millions to make a socialist revolution and conquer state power. A victorious outcome is not inevitable. *That depends on us*, the working class and its political vanguard."

During a lively question and answer session after Studer's report, one participant asked whether an SWP candidate elected to Congress would support the US government sending arms to Ukrainians.

"We have no quarrel with how Ukrainians get arms to defend themselves from Moscow's assaults," Studer said. "At the same time, the longstanding proletarian internationalist position of the communist movement is and remains, 'Not one man and not one penny for the US rulers and their war machine! No political confidence in the bosses' government!'"

The US rulers do nothing other than advance their own imperialist interests in everything they do. If they extend military aid, it comes with strings attached. What's more, growing layers of the US ruling class, as well as the rulers of France, Germany, Italy, and elsewhere, are maneuvering today to pressure the Ukrainian government to give in, settle with Moscow, and make substantial territorial and political concessions. These imperialist voices want to end a war they increasingly see as a threat to their own interests.

"Decisions about starting and stopping wars are class decisions. The only way forward for working people is to fight to unite the toilers in Russia and Ukraine—as well as in the United States and elsewhere—in an effort to reverse Moscow's invasion."

The family and women's rights

In 1973 the *Militant* hailed as a victory the US Supreme Court's *Roe v. Wade* decision overturning laws in forty-six states that restricted a woman's access to safe, legal abortion during the first three months of pregnancy.

"Fifty years of experience in the class struggle have taught us that judgment was wrong," said SWP leader Mary-Alice Waters in opening her conference report. "It soon became clear that the court edict set back the fight to repeal all laws criminalizing and restricting abortion."

The 1973 ruling—decided by the Supreme Court on *political*, not constitutional grounds—"short-circuited the momentum that was building in the political fight to win a majority of the working class, male and female, to support the unconditional decriminalization of abortion, as a precondition for women's equality." And to understand that ending women's status as the "second sex" is central "to the program the working class must fight for on the road to emancipation."

Nowhere was that road presented more clearly than by Frederick Engels, one of the founders of modern communism, Waters said. "True equality between men and women," he wrote in 1885, "can become a reality only when the exploitation of both by capital has been abolished, and private work in the home has been transformed into a public industry."

Access to abortion under medically safe conditions has sharply declined from its high point soon after the 1973 ruling, Waters said. The liberal middle-class leadership of groups like the National Organization for Women "became little more than electoral appendages of the Democratic Party, with little interest in questions confronting families in the working class and among other exploited toilers. At the same time, abortion opponents were allowed to grab 'the right to life' as their banner."

As opposed to sanctifying what has been from the start a bad Supreme Court edict, Waters said, "our starting point is that there can be no road to women's liberation without dealing with the broader social crises bearing down on the families of working-class women and addressing the challenges and responsibilities that fall heavily on women as the bearers of new life."

In the question and answer session later that day, one participant disagreed with Waters' assertion that an overturn of *Roe v. Wade* would be positive. She asked Waters what she meant in saying in her conference report that "the SWP is the party of life, not death."

We must answer those who give a 'pro-life' mantle to attacks on women's rights. The working-class party that fights for humanity's liberation is the party of life. We must take back that banner.

"Getting the *Roe* decision out of the way will create an opportunity for working people to have the discussion we need," Waters replied. "The job of the courts is not to impose legislation," as it did in this case, "but to uphold rights and protections that have been wrested from the ruling class in struggles going back to the Bill of Rights and before." The 1973 *Roe v. Wade* ruling was an obstacle to fighting for access to safe and secure abortions, which is just one part of the broader working-class fight for both women and men today, she said.

It's essential to "answer those who cloak their assaults on women's rights under a 'pro-life' mantle. The working-class party that fights for the liberation of humanity is a party of life. We must take back that banner as ours."

During her presentation, Waters noted crucial lessons from the socialist revolutions in Russia in 1917 and Cuba in 1959. The Bolshevik-led revolution "was the first oppor-

The center of the women's emancipation struggle isn't abortion. True equality between men and women can become a reality only when the exploitation of both by capital has been abolished.

TAMAR ROSENFELD/MILITANT

Left: New York, October 2022. Lea Sherman, New Jersey SWP candidate for Congress, campaigns at "Women's Wave" march. The party calls for annulment of all laws restricting abortion access and "No to population control!"

Below: Melbourne, Australia, September 2018. Childcare workers demonstrate for equal pay and government funding for early education.

Left: Charleston, West Virginia, February 1969. Union miners demand protections against black lung disease. Backing the demand with strikes, they won greater union control over safety and employer-funded health clinics not just for black lung victims but for all miners and their entire families.

Below: Havana, Cuba, 1990. Childcare center built by volunteer construction brigade during "Rectification process" initiated by Fidel Castro in 1986. Earlier economic plan treated centers as an undesirable "social expense." Volunteers built fifty-four new centers in city in less than a year. "Whenever someone says no to childcare centers," Castro said, "you can be sure a bureaucratic, reactionary concept is at work."

BOHEMIA

tunity for a government of the working class to lead a fight for women's equality."

She pointed to communist leader V.I. Lenin's description of the domestic slavery confronting women in Russia a century ago. Those degrading conditions will change, Lenin said, "only where and when an all-out struggle begins (led by the proletariat wielding state power) against this petty housekeeping, or rather when its *wholesale transformation into a large-scale socialist economy begins.*"

As fellow Bolshevik leader Leon Trotsky explained, that required providing apartments and rural dwellings with running water and electricity. It required schools, jobs, laundries, and childcare centers, eradicating illiteracy, and combating drunkenness and domestic violence.

Advances in the Soviet Union initiated under Lenin's leadership and defended by Trotsky were reversed by the Stalin-led counterrevolution, one of the greatest defeats the working class has ever faced, Waters said.

Drawing lessons from the Soviet experience in his 1936 book *The Revolution Betrayed*, Trotsky wrote, "You cannot 'abolish' the family, you have to replace it." That's a task, Waters said, that can only be advanced by eliminating capitalism's economic compulsion on which the family is founded.

Women in Cuba

The second great socialist revolution of the last century took place in Cuba. Fidel Castro and other revolutionary leaders were determined from the outset to deepen women's involvement in all aspects of social life, clearing away obstacles to their shouldering political responsibilities to advance the revolution. Fidel insisted that a woman's organization, what became the Federation of Cuban Women, be established to lead these efforts. Those enormous accomplishments are recorded in the book edited by Waters, *Women in Cuba: The Making of a Revolution within the Revolution.*

The center of the fight for women's emancipation today is not abortion, Waters concluded. It's the family. It's part of a course to advance "the working-class fight for state power—to create the material and social conditions that will enable women and men to realize the basic conditions of our humanity. That means full participation in social labor *and* the ability to make conscious decisions, benefiting from advances in medical science, related to reproduction as well as production.

"That's the road not only to the emancipation of the working class," she said, "but to eradicating the historical roots of women's oppression."

SWP's trade union work

SWP members are active in our unions and carry out work in the broader labor movement, Mary Martin, the party's trade union director, told the conference. "Workers are showing what we are capable of, as we expand solidarity with each other's struggles."

She pointed to several strikes over the last year by members of the Bakery, Confectionery, Tobacco Workers, and Grain Millers union at Frito-Lay, Nabisco, Kellogg's, and Jon Donaire. Workers fought to push back "suicide shifts" and "divorce shifts" that wreck family life, make it very difficult to take an active part in union and political activity, and endanger workers' health and safety. Some gains have been won and solidarity expanded.

The SWP has encouraged party members to get jobs in BCTGM-organized plants or in workplaces that can be or-

Left: Piccadilly station in Manchester, United Kingdom, October 2022, part of one-day strike across the UK by 160,000 rail, postal, and dockworkers to protest rising prices, worsening job conditions.

Right: Galesburg, Illinois, July 2022. Rail workers and supporters rally against refusal by bosses and government to address long, irregular hours; denial of sick days; and dangerous working conditions.

Through our unions we help mobilize solidarity with strikes and other struggles, reaching out to the broad labor movement.

Facing page: In Toronto, 55,000 members of the Canadian Union of Public Employees waged two-day strike in November 2022 over inflation-wracked wages and staffing in schools. Faced with strikes and wide solidarity, provincial government withdrew its draconian anti-strike law.

OSBORNE HART/MILITANT

Left: East Hempfield, Pennsylvania, October 2021. Members of bakery workers union struck Kellogg's over equal pay for equal work and opposition to two-tier pay and benefits system.

COURTESY OF JEFF SCHUHRKE

ganized into the union. The party has also expanded the kinds of jobs its members take in BCTGM-organized shops, opening up both union and political life to more of the party's cadres. At the same time, SWP members are working jobs organized by freight rail unions.

Martin reviewed some recent experiences in the unions. Party members have joined coworkers and others to expand backing for the United Mine Workers union, which has been on strike against Warrior Met Coal in Brookwood, Alabama, since April 2021.

We've helped win support among workers and farmers for a two-day strike by rail workers on the Canadian Pacific in March, as well as joining with other rail workers to put a spotlight on rising numbers of rail-yard deaths in recent years.

And we've gotten out the truth, through union channels and in the pages of the *Militant*, about the deaths this year of two bakery workers in nonunion jobs in North Carolina.

At the same time, SWP members carry out the party's propaganda campaigns among coworkers, as they join week in and week out in branch activity to expand the reach of the party's program among working people at their doorsteps, on picket lines, and at social protests and political meetings.

This trade union and political work described by Martin was followed up the last evening of the conference at a lively rally, with remarks by thirteen conference participants from the US, Canada, the UK, and New Zealand.

Maggie Trowe, a member of the Cincinnati branch, described the efforts she and her BCTGM coworkers organized there to back the Alabama miners at Warrior Met Coal.

John Hawkins, a party member from Chicago, talked about the work SWP members did recently to win support from working farmers in the US for a solidarity message to Cuban farmers on the sixty-third anniversary of Cuba's sweeping land reform and the sixty-first anniversary of the National Association of Small Farmers (ANAP). The worker-farmer alliance that made possible Cuba's socialist revolution was built on the bedrock of the land reform.

Osborne Hart, SWP candidate for US Senate from Pennsylvania, described the openings to use the campaign, including concentrated campaigning beginning right after the conference. The party there is petitioning to place the party's candidate, Chris Hoeppner, on the ballot for US Congress from Philadelphia. [The party won ballot status in August, after collecting and submitting well over twice the state signature requirement.]

The rally concluded with a fund appeal that raised $44,769 for the party's work, and a spirited singing of "The Internationale," the fighting anthem of the working class the world over.

"I especially enjoyed the class on Independent Working-Class Politics," Jacob Pirro from Montreal told the *Militant*. He was attending his first conference. "During the civil rights movement the US Communist Party told its members to help get Democrats into office."

"In contrast to the CP, Malcolm X and the SWP taught fighters for Black rights, 'Don't trust your oppressor.'" That same question faces fighters trying to change the world today, Pirro said.

"I want to learn more about the history of the SWP and its continuity going back to the Bolsheviks," said Vincent Auger from Seattle, also at his first party conference.

The day after the SWP conference, organized supporters of the communist movement from around the world met with party leaders to plan their coming year's work. The supporters' auxiliary organizes the production, printing, and distribution of Pathfinder books by SWP and other revolutionary leaders and systematically works to raise funds the SWP uses for its political and publishing work.

This year supporters organized a table in the auditorium to show participants the work they've done to carry out the party's proposal in late 2021 to begin formatting books for the blind and those with low vision in several accessible formats, from audio books to braille. It was one of the most visited displays at the conference.

Defend Ukraine's sovereignty and independence

Moscow's troops out now! US troops and nuclear arms out of Europe!

THE VLADIMIR PUTIN REGIME in Russia has unleashed a murderous war, an invasion of Ukraine accompanied by massive bombardment of civilian-occupied urban centers. In face of this intentional carnage, and despite Putin's dangerous and provocative action placing Moscow's nuclear forces on high alert, Ukrainians are fighting courageously, arms in hand, to defend Ukraine's national sovereignty and independence. The Socialist Workers Party hails their resistance and calls for the defeat of Putin's invading forces.

As the Stalinist regime in the Soviet Union collapsed in face of massive popular mobilizations at the beginning of the 1990s, Ukraine was one of fourteen former republics to declare national independence. Now Putin's regime is ruthlessly seeking to claw back, under Moscow's domination, those nations once incarcerated in the czarist prison house of nations, regenerating a Russian empire today with Putin as its czar.

This Socialist Workers Party National Committee statement was released March 3, 2022, by Jack Barnes, the party's national secretary.

Moscow's aim is "to erase our history, erase our country," as Ukrainian president Volodymyr Zelensky concisely expressed it March 1.

Putin insists Ukraine is not a nation and has no right to exist as one. "Modern Ukraine was entirely and fully created by Russia," he claims. It is "an inalienable part of our own [Russian] history, culture, and spiritual space." He proclaims that his hoped-for resurrection of the empire is a step toward rejuvenating Christendom, with its "Holy See" in the Russian Orthodox patriarchate of Moscow.

Russia's armed forces face tenacious resistance and have taken thousands of deaths and injuries in the first week of the assault. In face of these setbacks, Moscow's armed forces have now stepped up heavy bombardment of residential and commercial areas in hopes of sowing terror and cowing the Ukrainian people into submission. Russian planes and cruise missiles have struck apartment buildings, homes, schools, hospitals, and railway stations in Mariupol, Kharkiv, Kherson, Kyiv, and numerous smaller cities. Ukraine's State Emergency Service reported March 1 that two thousand civilians had been killed during the first week, as well as many Ukrainian soldiers.

Under Putin's direction, his high command is intensifying siege warfare against the population of Ukraine, cutting off electricity, water, sanitation, and cellphone, television, and radio communications.

In face of rising Jew-hating demagogy and violence in today's world, there is mounting disgust among Jews in Ukraine and beyond at the outrageous claims by Putin—himself a product of Russia's notoriously Jew-hating secret police, formerly called the KGB—that Moscow's aggression aims to "denazify" Ukraine.

Ukrainian president Zelensky is Jewish, with a grand-father who fought in the Soviet army to turn back the German imperialist invaders. Other family members were killed in the Holocaust. On March 2 "denazifying" Russian missiles struck a TV tower in Babyn Yar, the site of the slaughter of more than thirty thousand Jews by Nazi forces during World War II. A Jewish cemetery was desecrated. No wonder Jews around the world see more of the truth and are encouraging Jews in Ukraine who are joining with others there to stand and fight.

Russian soldiers and sailors are beginning to become demoralized and disillusioned. They've been lied to by Putin's regime about what to expect, being told they'd be welcomed as "liberators," and would quickly roll over Ukraine's military forces. Now they're not only taking substantial casualties but facing shortages of food and fuel. Some are disobeying orders to shell civilian targets; retreating from battle or surrendering without a fight; even sabotaging or abandoning Russian military equipment.

Inside Russia, tens of thousands have poured into the streets of cities and towns all across that vast country to demand a halt to the war. They are doing so in face of police repression, with more than seven thousand arrests the first week, as well as government threats of being charged with "treason." Street demonstrations are spreading across Europe, the Americas, and worldwide.

The Socialist Workers Party opposes the broadly aimed economic and financial embargo imposed on Russia by the US, European, and other imperialist ruling classes, as well as military maneuvers by these governments. Those sanctions ultimately fall most harshly on working people in Russia.

Washington and its capitalist allies in London, Paris, Berlin, and elsewhere shed crocodile tears over Ukraine's national sovereignty and the plight of its people. High-flown phrases aside, however, their only real concern is to protect their own profits and strategic political interests in the region. The Socialist Workers Party demands the withdrawal of all US troops and both conventional and nuclear arms and nuclear missile systems from NATO member countries in Europe!

Since the 1990s, both Democratic and Republican administrations and Congresses have acted to reinforce US imperialism's post-World War II position as the dominant "European" military power. In collaboration with other imperialist governments in Europe, as well as the other capitalist regimes involved, Washington has extended the reach of its armed might closer to Russia's borders. This includes deployment of ballistic missiles in Poland and Romania.

Putin's efforts to excuse his bloodthirsty invasion of Ukraine on grounds of moves by Washington and other NATO governments are as cynical as they are false. A sovereign and independent Ukraine poses no military threat to Russia of any kind.

At the same time, the Socialist Workers Party lends no political confidence to the capitalist government in Kyiv, which stands behind Ukraine's wealthy rulers in their pressure on the living and job conditions and political rights of coal miners, rail workers, farmers, and others among the oppressed and exploited.

The Socialist Workers Party stands and acts on our communist continuity with V.I. Lenin, under whose leadership the Bolshevik Party in October 1917 led the working class to state power in Russia. It was that revolutionary workers and peasants republic that ensured the right to self-determination to Ukraine and other oppressed nations formerly trapped within the czarist empire.

In 1922, after consolidating victory over the counterrevolutionary armies of the capitalists, landlords, and sixteen invading foreign powers, the Bolshevik-led government established a voluntary federation of the Russian, Ukrainian, and four other republics: the Union of Soviet Socialist Republics.

Communists in Russia, Lenin insisted, must "declare war to the death on Great Russian chauvinism." It was only after the counterrevolution led by Joseph Stalin against Lenin's proletarian internationalist course that Ukraine and other oppressed peoples were again denied their language, cultural, and other national rights.

Members and supporters of the Socialist Workers Party are campaigning to get out the truth about the Russian government's murderous assault on Ukraine's sovereignty, on its right to exist as a nation. We and fellow communists in other countries are getting this statement, along with weekly *Militant* coverage of the struggle of the Ukrainian people, into the hands of working people far and wide, including strike picket lines, social protests, at workers' doorsteps, and actions against Russia's invasion occurring across the United States and the world over.

The Socialist Workers Party is mobilizing its candidates for the US Senate, House of Representatives, and other public offices to use the 2022 election campaign to get out the truth and present an independent working-class foreign policy. A foreign policy that starts from the interests of the toilers at home and internationally—not from hypocritical chants about "democracy" and "freedom" behind which the capitalist rulers seek to mask their exploitation and oppression of billions the world over.

No political organization is more prepared to explain the stakes for working people in rolling back Moscow's invasion than the Socialist Workers Party.

JOHN STUDER/MILITANT

JOHN STUDER/MILITANT

CATHARINA TIRSEN/MILITANT

The *Militant* newsweekly made three reporting trips to Ukraine following the 2014 popular uprising that toppled the discredited pro-Moscow regime.

Above: Team visited Independence Square, Kyiv, March 2014. Trade Union House there had been burned out a month earlier as regime waged deadly attacks on protesters. **Inset:** Miner at Donetsk workers' tent in square reading *Militant*.

Below: *Militant* reporting team led by paper's editor, John Studer, holding pen, and Frank Forrestal, in black cap, talk to miners in Kryvyi Rih, eastern Ukraine, June 2015.

The stakes are enormous. Working people must see the necessity of taking political power into our own hands—as toilers did in Cuba at the opening of the 1960s, following a popular, workers-and-farmers-based revolution—or we will face a future of social devastation, reaction, world war, and even nuclear catastrophe.

Join us in this effort to raise an independent working-class voice in the United States—to have an impact on public opinion here, elsewhere in the Americas, Europe, and the world. Join us in demanding:

For the defeat of Moscow's murderous invasion and bombardment of Ukraine!

Defend Ukraine's independence and sovereignty!

Get Washington's nuclear weapons and armed forces out of Europe, *all* of Europe, now!

Demand Washington end its economic war against Cuba now!

THE SOCIALIST WORKERS PARTY DEMANDS that the US government end its sixty-three-year-long economic, trade, and financial war against the people of Cuba.

Immediately.

No strings attached.

This brutal policy has been carried out by *every one* of the thirteen Democratic and Republican administrations since 1959. The US rulers' aim has been to crush the spirit of Cuba's working people, the socialist revolution they made and have defended for more than six decades, and the example it sets for toilers in the United States, across the Americas and worldwide.

The cumulative toll of this all-encompassing imperialist assault has been magnified in recent weeks by the effects of Hurricane Ian, which damaged or demolished tens of thousands of homes and farms in western Pinar del Río and Artemisa provinces, contaminated water supplies, and

---

This Socialist Workers Party National Committee statement was released October 11, 2022, by Jack Barnes, the party's national secretary.

plunged most of the country into darkness for more than twenty-four hours.

This made-in-Washington social disaster comes on top of the raging petroleum fire August 5 in Matanzas, which destroyed half the storage capacity at Cuba's largest oil distribution facility. Due to longstanding trade bans and suffocating international banking sanctions, Cubans continue to face severe shortages of medicine and medical supplies, fuel, and other vital necessities. The impact of these imperialist measures is multiplied by exploding prices, rising interest rates, and stagflation due to world capitalism's production and trade crisis. And now by the consequences of the COVID pandemic and Moscow's invasion of Ukraine, as well.

For working people and our allies in the United States—which is the imperialist powerhouse of this unrelenting assault—there could be no more urgent time for every opponent of Washington's embargo to demand of the Biden White House and Congress: End the economic war against Cuba NOW! Every aspect of it. And forswear its reimposition!

There could be no better moment to explain the facts and win growing numbers of working people and youth to this decisive political battle.

Instead, the New York-based People's Forum placed a full-page "Urgent Appeal to President Biden" in the October 2 Sunday edition of the *New York Times* begging the Biden administration to *suspend* the embargo, *"even if just for the next six months,* to purchase the necessary construction materials to REBUILD" [italics added].

What a betrayal of the elementary obligation of those of us here in the United States who oppose Washington's assault on Cuban sovereignty. What a betrayal of the interests of working people on both sides of the Florida Straits.

Whatever our views on other issues, now is the time to come together in calling on Washington to immediately and unconditionally *end* the embargo. Not lift it for a few months. Not make it a bit more bearable, before the US rulers again inflict it.

End it!

For those living in the US to demand anything short of that lends political legitimacy to Washington's decades-long economic war against the Cuban Revolution. We demand that the US government halt every diplomatic and political manifestation of that hostile course as well.

The US imperialist rulers and their two political parties don't need advice on *how* to do so. They don't need lessons on the deaths and destruction caused by the embargo—*that's the rulers' aim,* and has been for more than six decades. As the State Department's infamous "Mallory memorandum" put it in April 1960: "The majority of Cubans support" the revolution. For the US government, therefore, the necessary state policy must be one that "makes the greatest inroads in denying money and supplies to Cuba, to decrease monetary and real wages, to bring about hunger, desperation, and overthrow of [the] government."

Cuban workers and farmers in arms rapidly put to rest Washington's goal of instigating the "overthrow of the government." Those efforts by the US rulers were dealt lasting political and military blows by Cuba's revolutionary militias, armed forces, and police in April 1961. The attempted invasion of Cuba at the Bay of Pigs by US-organized mercenaries was routed in less than seventy-two hours.

At a mobilization of hundreds of thousands in Havana to prepare to crush that aggression, Fidel Castro confirmed what Cuban toilers' own class-struggle experience had already taught them. "This is the socialist and democratic revolution of the working people, by the working people, and for the working people," Fidel said. "And for this revolution, we are prepared to give our lives."

Addressing President Biden, the People's Forum pleads: "The people of Cuba are part of our family—the human family. Don't let outdated Cold War politics prevent peace-loving people from helping the Cubans to rebuild.... The United States loses nothing by being a good neighbor and allowing Cuba to recover fully from this tragic moment."

But there's no such thing as a politically homogeneous "United States"; it's class divided. Unlike working people in this country, the propertied ruling families represented by the imperialist Democratic and Republican parties *have a great deal to lose* by "allowing Cuba to recover." That's why the Biden White House has doubled down on the most punishing package of sanctions yet imposed on Cuba. The capitalists hope their decades-long inhumane policy is working.

Their actions—ever since the subjugation of Cuba during the Spanish-American War at the dawn of the twentieth century—prove they don't care about "the human family." They care about raising profit rates and intensifying the exploitation of working people, whatever the consequences for *our* families.

Washington's course has nothing to do with "outdated Cold War politics." It has to do with Cuba's socialist revolution: with the example set by the workers and farmers who made that revolution and defend it to this day.

The US rulers are determined to bury that revolution in a mountain of lies and smother any political interest among workers and farmers in emulating what our brothers and sisters in Cuba have achieved. It's what the bosses try to do to every strike and struggle by working people in the United States itself.

Their hatred—and fear—of the working people of Cuba is in fact an extension of their contempt for workers here fighting to defend our constitutional freedoms against assaults by the White House, the FBI, and other institutions of repression of the capitalist state.

The US rulers fear rail workers, coal miners, bakery workers, and other working people organizing to strengthen our trade unions as we fight for safe job conditions, for wages that grow faster than inflation, and for shorter hours and work schedules that enable us to share in the lives of our families and take part in union, political, and cultural activity. They have contempt for tens of millions fighting exploitation, the oppression of African Americans and women, and the wars produced by capitalism's dog-eat-dog social relations.

When Cuban foreign minister Bruno Rodríguez was in New York in September to address the United Nations General Assembly, he was asked by an interviewer whether the Cuban government, in face of the imposition of hundreds of new US sanctions in recent years, would "negotiate anything with America ever again."

"We will have to," the foreign minister pointed out, as the Cuban government has always done when there's an opening "to reestablish dialogue" on the basis of mutual sovereignty and respect.

Cuban diplomatic personnel press for every advance in this direction they can wrench through talks with Washington and other governments regarding the brutal embargo,

Cuba's removal from the contemptible "State Sponsors of Terrorism" list, the status of occupied Cuban territory at Guantánamo, migration issues, drug trafficking, and environmental disasters.

That's the obligation of the Cuban government to the Cuban people, an obligation Cuba's foreign ministry has met with dignity and honor since the first days of the revolution.

Opponents in the US of Washington's brutal course must never give an inch, not even the tip of a finger, to the rulers' decades-long assaults on Cuba's sovereignty.

The responsibility of the working-class movement and others in this country who defend Cuba's national sovereignty and independence, however, is not the same. It is Washington, which falsely claims to speak in the name of the people of the United States, that has waged a nonstop assault on the Cuban Revolution since 1959. Contrary to the proposals in the *New York Times* ad, our job—the job of opponents here in the United States of Washington's brutal, reactionary course—is to never give an inch, even the tip of a finger, to the US rulers' encroachment on Cuba's sovereignty.

The revolutionary program, confidence, proletarian conduct, and activity of the Socialist Workers Party have been renewed and strengthened over decades by the steadfastness of Cuban working people and the Cuban government in defending what they've conquered. Both in word and above all in deeds, we will continue getting out the truth about their socialist revolution to working people in the US and wherever else we can reach.

End Washington's economic, trade, financial, and diplomatic war against the people of Cuba!

Now!

The low point of labor resistance is behind us

SOCIALIST WORKERS PARTY RESOLUTION

I.

Opposing US rulers' assaults on freedoms protected by the Constitution and their use of the political police

1) Defending and extending the freedoms protected by the US Constitution is at the center of the class struggle today. Workers and farmers must organize and act to prevent the federal government's assault on these freedoms, which we have won in class battles over some two and a half centuries. We must oppose the US rulers' relentless drive to refurbish the reputation and expand the use of the government's political police, first and foremost the FBI.

The political course of the current Democratic administration includes an open assault on these very freedoms. Employing violent and provocative demagogy, President Biden, in his September 1, 2022, "Battle for the Soul of the Nation" speech in Philadelphia, condemned as "a threat to this country" tens of millions of US citizens who voted for former President Donald Trump in 2020 or who would have done so if they had the chance (74 million people cast

Socialist Workers Party National Committee Political Resolution, adopted by the 49th Constitutional Convention of the SWP, December 12, 2022.

ballots for him). The "MAGA Republicans," Biden said, are carrying out an "ongoing attack on democracy." They represent "a clear and present danger," he warned, "an extremism that threatens the very foundations of our republic."

A week earlier, Biden had branded "MAGA Republicans" as "semi-fascists." There is no rise of fascism in the US today, but Biden's Philadelphia performance did call up images of Nuremberg rallies. It was staged against the backdrop of garish red lighting, with two active duty Marines in uniform flanking an American flag. In defiance of government and US Armed Forces policy against uniformed soldiers being used at political events, the Democratic administration mobilized Marine sentries and had the Marine Band play "Hail to the Chief" as Biden walked to the podium. The talk was so flagrantly a political event, not a presidential address to the nation, that all television networks but two (MSNBC and CNN) refused White House requests to broadcast it live. Even more, Biden's speech posed a brazen threat to the people's constitutional rights.

Class-conscious workers, the trade unions, and organizations of the oppressed and exploited must unconditionally oppose anti-constitutional assaults by the government on freedom of worship and speech; freedom of the press, association, and assembly; prohibition of "unreasonable search and seizure"; and other liberties needed and *used* by the toilers.

That's true whether the target is a former US president; a football coach who takes a knee to pray; a family persecuted for publicly affirming their religious beliefs and practices; leaders of a small Black nationalist organization; a Cuba solidarity committee; fighters for Puerto Rican in-

Defending the freedoms protected by the Constitution is at the center of the class struggle in the United States today.

Above: President Joseph Biden, speaking September 2022 in Philadelphia, flanked by Marine honor guard. Biden condemned tens of millions of US residents—"MAGA Republicans," he called them—as a "clear and present danger" to the "foundations of our republic."

Below: Palm Beach, Florida, August 2022. Biden's "Justice" Department stages armed raid on home of former president Donald Trump, trampling constitutional protections against unreasonable searches and seizures of people's homes and belongings.

"Under the bourgeois regime, all suppression of political rights and freedom, no matter whom they are directed against in the beginning, in the end inevitably bear down upon the working class," wrote communist leader Leon Trotsky in 1939.

"We stand for freedom of speech and assembly in principle. Not just for us, but for everybody."

— Farrell Dobbs, SWP national secretary, 1961

PHOTOS: ARNOLD WEISSBERG/MILITANT

Above: New York, October 2022. Meeting at People's Church in East Harlem condemns FBI harassment of some 60 Puerto Ricans who visited Cuba on solidarity trip. **Inset:** Rev. Dorlimar Lebrón welcomes participants.

AFRICAN PEOPLE'S SOCIALIST PARTY

Above: In July 2022, FBI commandos broke into homes and offices of African People's Socialist Party in St. Louis (above) and St. Petersburg, Florida. They detained leaders of group at gunpoint, accusing them of being "agents" of Moscow. As of late 2022, none have been indicted.

dependence; a striking United Mine Workers local or embattled union rail workers; farmers indicted for grazing livestock on public lands; a speaker, author, or teacher "canceled" by the "woke"; prisoners denied the *Militant* newsweekly and other reading material; or Socialist Workers Party candidates.

Whoever the target today, it is working people who will be targeted tomorrow.

"We stand for freedom of speech and assembly in principle—not just for us, but for everybody," insisted Farrell Dobbs in the Political Report adopted by the June 1961 SWP convention, reaffirming longtime party policy.

In August 2022 the Biden administration's "Justice Department" staged a nine-hour raid on former president Trump's Florida home, carried out by more than thirty FBI and Secret Service agents, many of them heavily armed. Long experience has taught class-conscious workers that when the government, in a violent or threatening manner, takes aim at a rival capitalist politician or party, the same methods and worse have been and will again be used by the rulers to harass and disrupt union battles, struggles by working farmers, opponents of Washington's wars, fighters for Black liberation, and communists.

As Leon Trotsky forcefully reminded us in 1939, "Under conditions of the bourgeois regime, all suppression of political rights and freedom, no matter whom they are directed against in the beginning, in the end inevitably bear down upon the working class, particularly its most advanced elements. That is a law of history."

2) In September 1939 the Democratic Party administration of Franklin Roosevelt issued a "Presidential Directive" to ensure "the internal safety of our country." That execu-

tive order initiated a transformation of the FBI, which up to then had been a federal police force pursuing interstate law-breaking, financial fraud, and organized crime, a force most of whose field agents were lawyers or accountants. It was reborn as *a federal political police* acting at the behest of the president, whichever party occupied the White House. Its agents carried arms as a matter of course. The FBI was now aimed above all at stabilizing and preserving the capitalist state, as preparations accelerated for the US rulers to take the country into the expanding imperialist slaughter.

Long-established "red squads," "bomb squads," and "radical units" of state and local police departments, as well as company goons and other private security forces, were no longer sufficient to the global needs of US finance capital. Even under conditions of bourgeois democracy, the imperialist ruling class, whose executive committee sits in Washington, must have a national political police able to operate secretly and largely with impunity. During World War II the FBI was in charge of counterintelligence, and after 1945 it competed with the newly established Central Intelligence Agency and National Security Agency in counterespionage operations.

Roosevelt's 1939 executive order instructed the FBI "to take charge of" investigations related to "espionage," "counterespionage," "neutrality laws," and, most importantly for the working class, what his administration called "subversive activities." The latter was an undefined and elastic term calculated to include militant trade unionism, independent working-class political action, and, above all, any determined opposition to the US rulers' entry into the second imperialist world war.

Under bourgeois democracy, the imperialist ruling class needs a national political police able to operate secretly and largely with impunity.

Above: Democratic president Franklin Roosevelt, signs 1934 bill, a forerunner to 1939 executive order increasing FBI powers to target labor movement and "subversives." FBI director, J. Edgar Hoover is directly behind Roosevelt.

Below: Raid on Socialist Workers Party headquarters in Minneapolis, June 1941. Roosevelt administration aimed to silence working-class forces campaigning in the labor movement against US rulers' preparations to send young workers, farmers, and others into the imperialist war.

The same month Roosevelt signed the executive order, the New Deal White House unleashed the freshly minted political police against the rising class-struggle leadership of the working class. FBI agents in Nebraska and Iowa raided the homes of union militants in Omaha, Des Moines, and Sioux City who were leaders of the Teamsters Midwest over-the-road organizing drive. Framed up on charges of transporting a stolen truck across state lines and burning it, seven Teamsters leaders were railroaded to federal prison. It was an unmistakable warning to the most advanced layers of the US working class.

By 1942, soon after Washington's formal entry into the war, the FBI was getting regular reports about union and political activity from some twenty-four thousand informers in four thousand factories, mines, and mills across the US. The Minneapolis-based Teamsters organizing drive and their leaders were central targets of this massive undercover operation.

FBI agents organized snitches and provocateurs in Teamsters Local 544 to slander and frame up central leaders of the unionization drive. Many of those trade unionists were leading cadres of the Socialist Workers Party. In June 1941 the FBI raided the SWP's public headquarters, libraries, and bookstores in Minneapolis and in St. Paul, accompanied by reporters and photographers from the cities' main dailies and national wire services. The federal cops seized cartons of books, pamphlets, issues of the *Militant*, and other publications. This "search and seizure," carried out in violation of the Constitution, was sensationalized across front pages the next day.

In July 1941 Roosevelt's Justice Department handed down indictments against twenty-nine SWP and Local 544 leaders. The government's aim was to cripple the unionization drive and behead the developing class-struggle union leadership. Above all it aimed to silence the forces in the labor movement campaigning to a growing working-class audience against the US rulers' rationalizations for dragging them into the unfolding imperialist war being fought from the Atlantic to the Pacific.

The indictment had two counts: (1) "conspiracy to overthrow the government by force and violence," in violation of the 1861 Seditious Conspiracy Act, originally aimed at leaders of the secessionists who soon formed the Confederate States of America; and (2) "conspiracy *to advocate* [emphasis added] the overthrow of the government by force and violence." The thought-control Smith Act, under which the second count was lodged, had been signed into law by Roosevelt only months earlier in 1940. It was used by the government for the first time in this frame-up. All those indicted were acquitted on the seditious conspiracy charge. Eighteen were convicted under the "conspiracy to advocate" clause of the Smith Act and sent to prison on sentences of up to sixteen months.

The Socialist Workers Party, through the *Militant* and other avenues, took the political lead in getting the truth out to working people, the labor movement, and beyond about the anti-working-class purpose and anti-constitutional activities of the newly consolidated political police. This included the party's initiative in launching the Civil Rights Defense Committee to wage an international defense campaign to combat the frame-up and win freedom for those imprisoned. Organized in the midst of World War II, the campaign won broad support in the unions and from Black rights and other organizations, despite vicious opposition from the Communist Party and the labor, Black, and civil rights groups it influenced.

3) In the 1960s, 1970s and 1980s, the SWP again broke new ground in combating government assaults on constitutional rights through our political campaign and federal lawsuit against the FBI, US Attorney General, and other political police agencies.

With the rise of the "Cold War" after World War II, Washington escalated its use of informers, harassment tactics, break-ins, phone taps, and other unconstitutional methods. Among those the government targeted were the rising proletarian-based movement to smash Jim Crow segregation, as well as Malcolm X and numerous Black liberation organizations; those demanding fair play for Cuba and organizing solidarity with Cuba's socialist revolution; participants in and leaders of the fight to end US imperialism's war against the Vietnamese people, including citizen-soldiers exercising their constitutional rights; militant trade unionists and labor struggles; and the emerging fight for women's emancipation.

The SWP was actively involved in all these struggles. Moreover, as we had done from our communist origins in 1919, we distinguished ourselves as principled and uncompromising defenders of all targets of government frame-ups.

In 1949 eleven Communist Party leaders were tried and convicted in federal court under the Smith Act. This was the very same repressive legislation that only a few years earlier had been used by the Roosevelt administration—cheered on by the CP leadership—to railroad to prison leaders of the Midwest Teamsters and the SWP. Farrell Dobbs, who became national secretary of the SWP in 1953, covered on the scene the nine-month frame-up trial week in and week out for the *Militant*, and we campaigned for the release of the CP leaders after their imprisonment for the maximum sentence of five years.

In the mid-1960s the SWP championed a successful four-year-long effort to defend three members of the Young Socialist Alliance in Bloomington, Indiana, indicted under the state Anti-Communism Act in May 1963 for "assembling" during the October 1962 "Cuban missile crisis" to advocate the overthrow of the State of Indiana by force and violence.

The FBI launched undercover disruption operations—so-called Cointelpro programs—against the Socialist Workers Party and Young Socialist Alliance, the Communist Party, Black rights organizations, Chicano and Mexicano groups, American Indian militants, and many others. Opponents of government policies were fired from jobs and evicted from apartments. FBI agents instigated and fomented factional divisions, "agent baiting," and race-baiting within and among groups susceptible to such dirty tricks, leading to expulsions, splits, and sometimes beatings or murders.

In flagrant defiance of the Fourth Amendment's guarantees against "unreasonable search and seizure," the FBI conducted pervasive wiretapping and opened mail of targeted organizations and individuals. The FBI acknowledged in court more than two hundred burglaries of Socialist Workers Party offices ("black bag jobs," in thuggish FBI lingo), and admitted that the agency had collected ten million pages of files on the SWP and on its members.

Federal District Judge Thomas Griesa's 1986 decision in the lawsuit filed by the SWP and YSA against Washington's political police concluded that the government had produced "no evidence that any FBI informant ever reported an instance of planned or actual espionage, violence, [or] terrorism" by the party or any of its members. The judge ruled that the FBI's use of undercover informers, its Cointelpro operations, and its "black bag jobs" were "violations of the constitutional rights of the SWP and lacked legislative or regulatory authority."

The SWP's victory helped keep political space open for all to speak, organize, and act. Especially on the party's working-class terrain—the factories, fields, and mines; in picket lines, the streets, and soldiers' barracks.

The party's campaign and the victory won for the SWP and YSA helped keep political space open for all working people to speak, organize, and act—not only with respect to the electoral and judicial arenas, but also the party's own working-class terrain: in factories, fields, and mines; at picket lines and on the streets; at bull sessions in soldiers' barracks; and at political events and social protests of all kinds. In short, wherever the exploited and oppressed classes are thinking politically, discussing, and fighting back.

Another exposure of FBI trampling on constitutional guarantees of our freedoms had been made twelve years earlier, in a 1974 federal Department of Justice memorandum written by Antonin Scalia, an assistant attorney general who later served on the US Supreme Court. Scalia was the most influential, and useful, Supreme Court justice of the latter twentieth century and opening fifteen years of the twenty-first. The FBI had rejected a Freedom of Information Act (FOIA) request by SWP member Morris Starsky to receive secret Cointelpro documents relevant to the fight against his politically motivated firing as a professor at Arizona State University.

Scalia recommended to the Justice Department that the FBI's objections be overruled. He pointed out that one requested document was an anonymous letter from a "concerned alumnus" fingering Starsky as an SWP member, aimed at "discrediting him in his academic community." Citing "national defense" prerogatives, the FBI had also rejected other requests by Starsky's attorney. But the agency did so, Scalia wrote, "without any indication or suspicion that [Starsky] obtained any defense secrets or had any connection whatever with foreign powers."

"In the last analysis," Scalia concluded, "the only policy reason for withholding most of the requested documents is to prevent a citizen from discovering the existence of possible misconduct and abuse of government power directed against him. In my view, this is not only no reason for asserting the exemption; it is a positive reason for declining to use it.... The obtaining of information of this sort is perhaps the most important reason for which the Freedom of Information Act exists."

4) Democrats, liberals, the "left," and "woke," so-called social justice warriors—not rightist or other reactionary forces—have led the assault against constitutional protections and freedoms in recent decades.

The Clinton White House established the first federal "counterintelligence czar." In the wake of 9/11, this paved the way for what is now called the Director of National Intelligence, centralizing federal political police operations spanning the FBI, CIA, military intelligence, and other agencies. To cite just a few among many measures undermining constitutional freedoms, the Clinton administration's 1994 Crime Bill eroded Fourth Amendment "search and seizure" safeguards, and in 1996 imposed its Anti-Terrorism and Effective Death Penalty Act—"Effective Death Penalty"!—which introduced "preventive detention" and use of "secret evidence."

Clinton's Justice Department led the cover-up of the murderous 1992 assault by FBI and ATF (Bureau of Alcohol, Tobacco and Firearms) sharpshooters on a family at Ruby Ridge in Idaho. During a standoff late in the George H. W. Bush administration, the unarmed mother (holding a baby in her arms) and her teenage son were shot and killed. As for the father, who was wounded by FBI snipers, all charges were later dropped except for failure to appear for a court date (the pretext for the massive armed assault). The Clinton White House followed up the next year with its own FBI siege and assault on the compound of the Branch Davidian religious group, resulting in the slaughter of more than eighty people near Waco, Texas.

In 1998 the Clinton administration ordered predawn FBI raids on the south Florida homes of the Cuban Five— Gerardo Hernández, Ramón Labañino, Antonio Guerrero, Fernando González, and René González—framing them up and sending them to federal prison on charges including conspiracy to commit espionage and, in one case, conspiracy to commit murder. Two years later, the administration unconstitutionally deployed 131 Immigration and Naturalization Service agents and twenty US marshals, many armed with assault weapons, for a middle-of-the-night raid on a private home in Miami. These federal commandos forcibly seized six-year-old Elián González, whom Washington had previously been refusing to return to his father's custody in Cuba.

That military-style operation "dealt a stunning blow to the right of every US resident to be 'secure in their persons, houses, papers, and effects, against unreasonable searches and seizures,' as provided by the US Constitution's Fourth Amendment," declared a front-page *Militant* editorial that week. "Every step taken by the US ruling class to close political space for working people within the United States...is a blow against the Cuban Revolution as well."

Following the initiatives of the Clinton White House, the Obama administration expanded internet and phone wiretapping, resurrecting the 1917 Espionage Act to spy on the Associated Press, a Fox News reporter, and other journalists and government "whistle-blowers."

In 2016 the Democratic administration, in collusion with like-minded FBI officials and Hillary Clinton campaign operatives, fabricated and paid for salacious slanders that Trump was a pawn of Moscow, lies they continued to spread during Trump's term in the White House and since.

And in 2010 and 2011, also during the Obama administration, the FBI raided the private homes of individuals in Chicago, Minneapolis, and Los Angeles in connection with "investigations" of the Freedom Road Socialist Organization and other groups; prosecutors' threats of indictments and Grand Jury inquisitions were baseless and soon collapsed.

Under the Biden administration there have been FBI raids and seizures of documents and electronic devices from individuals associated with Donald Trump and his presidential campaigns. There have also been FBI raids connected to investigations of the so-called January 6 insurrection.

And just days before the Mar-a-Lago operation, there were FBI raids against the Uhuru movement and the African People's Socialist Party on charges of being agents of Russia. Those assaults were followed a few weeks later by attempted FBI interrogations of some sixty people in Puerto Rico who had taken part in a solidarity brigade to Cuba.

Sharpening conflicts over race-baiting, Jew-hatred, "gender ideology," freedom of speech and worship express not just divisions in bourgeois politics. They ultimately reflect class divisions.

---

5) The sharpening political and social conflicts in the US over race-baiting, Jew-hatred, "gender ideology," freedom of religious expression, Second Amendment rights, vaccinations, school curricula, "cancel culture," immigration, and other matters are not only an expression of divisions in bourgeois politics between Democrats and Republicans, "conservative Red states" and "liberal Blue states," or "left" and "right." Whatever the camouflage, they ultimately reflect *class divisions*.

This class polarization is accelerating under the impact of US and world capitalism's profit-driven crises of production and trade. As the obscene wealth of the Gateses, Zuckerbergs, Waltons, and Musks grows, to say nothing of the Rockefellers, Mellons, DuPonts, and other longtime ruling-class families, the deterioration of living and job conditions

The percent of men in the United States holding a job has declined since the 1950s. Real wages have stagnated for half a century...

Percent of men in US with a job, 1960–2022

Share of men ages 25–54 who hold a job has dropped from 97 percent in 1960 to 88 percent today. St. Louis Federal Reserve Bank.

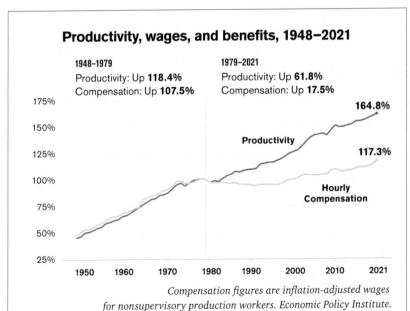

Productivity, wages, and benefits, 1948–2021

1948-1979
Productivity: Up **118.4%**
Compensation: Up **107.5%**

1979-2021
Productivity: Up **61.8%**
Compensation: Up **17.5%**

164.8%

Productivity

117.3%

Hourly Compensation

Compensation figures are inflation-adjusted wages for nonsupervisory production workers. Economic Policy Institute.

...Life expectancy in the US has declined to the lowest level in a quarter century. The birthrate has been cut in half since 1950. There's no mystery why working people are searching for answers.

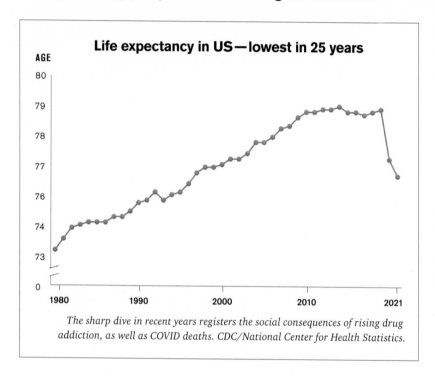

Life expectancy in US—lowest in 25 years

The sharp dive in recent years registers the social consequences of rising drug addiction, as well as COVID deaths. CDC/National Center for Health Statistics.

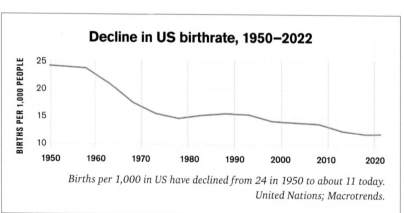

Decline in US birthrate, 1950–2022

Births per 1,000 in US have declined from 24 in 1950 to about 11 today.
United Nations; Macrotrends.

of working people and our families undercuts all pretense that "a rising tide lifts all boats."

In the wake of billions of dollars of pandemic handouts, as well as sharp reductions in capitalist investment, production, and trade, the prices of food, fuel, housing, health care, and other necessities are rising (boats no, prices yes!). An extended period of stagflation, combining inflation with stagnating capitalist production and hiring, is increasingly likely both in the US and worldwide.

Even the share of workers in the US who are part of the workforce—that is, those who hold down a job or are looking for work—has declined since the late 1990s. For men between the ages of twenty-five and fifty-four, this so-called labor-force participation rate has fallen sharply, from 97 percent in 1960 to 88 percent today. Real wages, adjusted for inflation, have stagnated since the 1970s. The birth rate is falling. Life expectancy in the US has declined to seventy-six years, its lowest level in more than a quarter century.

Exploited farmers face skyrocketing prices for fuel, seed, fertilizer, equipment, and other supplies. At the same time, reaping vast profits from land speculation, capitalists—from the likes of superrich "philanthropist" Bill Gates, to wealthy farmers and agricultural corporations—buy up more and more farm acreage, driving up land prices and preventing small farmers from obtaining enough to be economically viable. Much of this accumulation has occurred under the guise of promoting "environmental protection."

State and federal regulatory bureaus, such as water boards, groundwater agencies, the US Environmental Protection Agency, and various environmental bodies on state and local levels, increasingly tighten restrictions on access to water to the benefit of large-scale capitalist agriculture.

Working farmers are pushed deeper into debt and often off the land entirely. Ranchers have no choice but to sell off all or part of their herds. Available water in rural communities, especially in drought-stricken areas, is vastly depleted, leaving many with wells gone dry. Every opportunity to drive a wedge between exploited producers on the land and working people in cities and small towns is promoted.

Working farmers face skyrocketing prices for fuel, seed, and fertilizer, as well as tighter restrictions on access to water. They're pushed deeper into debt, and often forced off the land.

Working people the world over confront either comparably declining conditions, or much worse in the oppressed countries of Asia, Africa, the Middle East, Latin America, and the Caribbean.

Neither we nor anyone else can predict the direction of economic trends immediately ahead, or exactly how the class struggle will unfold. Amid inevitable cycles of capitalist business and trade, however, economic upturns will affect the working class, bolstering confidence and readiness to struggle. We've seen examples of this fact in the post-pandemic strikes and union struggles in the US, as we did during slumps and recoveries in the Great Depression of the 1930s.

What we do know is that whatever happens in capitalist economic and social life and the class struggle, our political course and program remain unchanged. Through building the unions and our conduct as unionists together with all other union members, we will respond to and advance the interests of our class and all the exploited.

6) Political and military alignments—"spheres of influence" that had shaped the global imperialist order since Washington emerged as the dominant power coming out of World War II—are being shaken and new alliances between competing states put together. Working people the world over are hit by the effects of growing global conflicts over trade, currency, raw materials, and immigration.

The first full-scale war between two state powers on the European continent in more than seventy-five years is now raging. Ignited by the assault of the secret-police-based capitalist regime of Vladimir Putin against Ukraine's national sovereignty and independence, that still-unfolding war has consequences that are only beginning to be registered worldwide.

Moscow's invasion of Ukraine, and the economic, political, and military shifts and uncertainties it creates, are temporarily overshadowing other "great power" conflicts, such as the long-smoldering confrontation between China and the US-led imperialist governments in the Pacific.

Tehran's expansionist drive to extend the bourgeois clerical regime's military and economic domination across the Middle East continues to pose the threat of an expanded conflagration. These perils are multiplied by the Iranian capitalist rulers' declared aim of eliminating the State of Israel, home to nearly half the world's Jews. Tehran's accelerated course toward developing and deploying a strategic nuclear arsenal endangers all those throughout the region and beyond.

The most important curb to this danger is Iran's working people—of Persian, Kurdish, Azerbaijani, Arab, and other

The drive by Tehran's capitalist rulers to extend their domination across the Middle East poses a constant threat of an expanded conflagration. Iran's working people are the greatest curb to this war danger.

Above: October 26, 2022, crowd at cemetery in Saqqez, Kurdish region of Iran, protests death of Zhina Amini in hands of Tehran's hated "morality" police. Despite fierce repression, Iran's rulers have been unable to push working people out of politics.

Below: Northern Iran, October 2022. Tehran regime carries out "Mighty Iran" military drill, near border with Azerbaijan. Government uses military and economic power to expand counterrevolutionary reach across the region.

national origins—who have protested in massive numbers in cities, villages, and rural areas in 2018, 2019, and again in 2022, in defiance of the regime and *all* its wings.

Workers, farmers, women, and youth are demanding affordable prices for food and fuel. An end to oppressive dress codes for women, enforced by the "morality" police. Language rights and other freedoms for oppressed nationalities. Restitution of unpaid wages, and protection of water rights. The freedom to speak their minds, organize, and act in their own class interests. They want no more of Tehran's counterrevolutionary military adventures across Iraq, Syria, Yemen, Lebanon, and beyond. No more body bags, funerals, and sacrifice at working people's expense and the enrichment of Iran's capitalist rulers.

7) Increasing class polarization and instability across the imperialist world order drive home the accuracy of the assessment in the party's 1990 convention resolution, "US Imperialism Has Lost the Cold War," that the collapse of the counterrevolutionary Stalinist regime in the Soviet Union would not bring about "a lessening danger of the use of nuclear weapons."

To the contrary, the resolution pointed out, the more governments that possess nuclear arsenals, "and the more class, national, and state conflicts intensify the world over, the greater the dangers that one of these capitalist regimes will resort to the use of nuclear weapons in the face of extreme pressure."

The possibility of the use of weapons of mass destruction in today's world can be seen not only in Tehran's drive to develop nuclear arms and delivery systems. Such a prospect is also underscored by Putin's nuclear saber rattling, in face of growing setbacks to his regime's efforts to crush Ukraine's national independence and sovereignty.

The Moscow regime confronts mounting battlefield defeats; demoralization and disaffection among its troops; opposition from wide layers of working people and the middle classes at home; and antagonism, overt and covert, among bourgeois rivals atop Russia's largest enterprises (who are cut off from profitable trade and financial markets) and within the state apparatus itself.

The governments of China, India, Turkey, and even Belarus are publicly taking greater distance from Putin, as are the governments of the Central Asian and South Caucasian republics, which gained independence from the disintegrating Soviet Union in 1991. None of the former Soviet republics in Asia and the Caucasus have recognized Putin's "annexations" in Ukraine.

In Asia and the Pacific, there will be growing consequences to Biden's repeated avowals (not "flubs") that Washington will respond militarily to any aggression by Beijing seeking to impose its direct dominance over Taiwan. As this confrontation escalates, the regime in China has cracked down harshly on political opposition in Hong Kong, and on the predominantly Muslim Uighur minority in China's Xinjiang Uighur Autonomous Region. It has fortified armed outposts on Pacific island chains claimed by other Asian regimes, from imperial Japan to Vietnam, the Philippines, and others.

And Washington maintains its deployment of some 28,000 troops and massive armaments in South Korea and is stepping up joint military maneuvers with Seoul, targeting the nuclear-armed government of the Democratic People's Republic of Korea.

In the decades since Washington unleashed atomic bombs on the people of Hiroshima and Nagasaki, the par-

Moscow's assault on Ukraine's national sovereignty has consequences worldwide that are only beginning to be registered. Including in Russia itself.

Top: Residents gather with Ukrainian flags, chanting "Kherson is Ukraine!" against Moscow's occupation forces, March 2022. Eight months later, Kherson was liberated.

Middle: Makhachkala, Dagestan, September 2022. Angry mothers gather in city center shouting, "No to war! No to mobilization!" in one of many protests across Russia, where young men have been forcibly conscripted off the streets.

Bottom: In early November 2022, Russian conscript soldiers confront general (in hat) at Kazan base chanting, "Shame on you!" "Let's go home!"

ty's 1990 convention resolution notes, the US rulers considered using nuclear weapons several times but decided not to. Washington publicly weighed such an option during the Korean War (newly liberated China would also have been a target); during the murderous, decade-long assault on the Vietnamese freedom struggle; as well as against the Cuban Revolution in its opening years.

"Only socialist revolutions in the imperialist countries can bring the danger of a world nuclear conflagration to an end once and for all," the 1990 SWP resolution states. That requires building "a revolutionary working-class movement powerful enough to overthrow the US capitalist rulers and disarm them," which in turn "requires a course toward building a proletarian communist party as part of a world communist movement."

No nonproliferation zones, arms limitation treaties, or diplomatic pacts between imperialist powers and other nuclear-armed regimes can or will advance the fight to stop the global spread and eventual use of such weapons. Nor will the call for unilateral nuclear disarmament of Washington and other governments. No propertied ruling class is going to disarm and risk its own wealth and power, while its competitors and enemies remain nuclear-armed to the teeth.

"*Disarmament'?*" asks our 1938 founding resolution, the Transitional Program, drafted by Leon Trotsky. "But the entire question revolves around who will disarm whom. The only disarmament which can avert or end war is the disarmament of the bourgeoisie by the workers." That became more true, not less, with the advent of nuclear weapons.

As communists and other class-conscious workers organize to advance a revolutionary struggle for workers power in the United States, our guide on these political and programmatic questions, as with many others, is the Transitional Program, including its section, "The struggle against imperialism and war."

"Not one man and not one penny" for the imperialist government, its budget, and its war machine, states our program, summing up one central aspect of our proletarian internationalist continuity from the Bolsheviks under Lenin to this day.

As Lenin wrote in the article "The 'Disarmament' Slogan" in 1916: "Only *after* the proletariat has disarmed the bourgeoisie will it be able, without betraying its world-historic mission, to consign all armaments to the scrap-heap." *All*, for us, includes conventional *and* nuclear weapons.

8) Amid the social and political crises driven by the laws of capital, the importance of the US working class safeguarding and *using* the freedoms and protections recognized and enumerated in the US Constitution is posed ever more clearly.

Bourgeois and upper-middle-class political forces, organized especially in the imperialist Democratic Party today, are seeking to disenfranchise those the liberals and the "left" scorn as benighted working people, whom they increasingly fear, as well. Dubbed "irredeemables" and "deplorables" by Hillary Clinton during the 2016 presidential election, these workers, farmers, and others are often today called "the MAGA Republican voters"—thus vastly and magically increasing their numbers into the tens of millions.

Proposals by the "enlightened" meritocracy and their hangers-on to eviscerate or even abolish the US Senate and

"Only socialist revolution in the imperialist countries can bring the danger of a world nuclear conflagration to an end once and for all."
— *Socialist Workers Party 1990 resolution*

Above: Demonstration by women in Petrograd, Russia, March 1917. Banner reads: "Comrade workers and soldiers, support our demands!"

Below: Workers militia on patrol at arms factory, south of Moscow, October 1917. With the Bolshevik Revolution of October 1917, the workers and peasants government immediately pulled Russia out of the first imperialist war, releasing publicly the secret treaties of all the rival capitalist plunderers of the world.

Electoral College are being openly voiced within the Democratic Party and its "progressive," "democratic socialist," and assorted radical and "woke" wings. Such schemes remain unlikely to succeed, since they require amending the Constitution. What appears more in reach to many liberals, however, is seeking to entrench four more "safe seat" Democratic US Senators, as well as several additional congresspeople, by imposing statehood on Puerto Rico and Washington, DC.

So does manipulating or packing the courts to hand over more and more *law-making* to unelected judges, proposals that also have support among many Democratic Party "progressives." The aim is to nullify the political voice and influence of working people in what many liberals and the left disdain as "flyover country." To sideline those "bitter" people in "small towns," who, in the words of Barack Obama, "cling to guns or religion or antipathy toward people who aren't like them."

It's with similar goals in mind that liberal middle-class layers have also gained yardage in increasing the unconstitutional policy-making and enforcement authority of government regulatory agencies and administrative bureaucracies, with their staffs of "experts," technocrats, and often their own specialized police forces. These span from the Internal Revenue Service to the National Labor Relations Board, from the Environmental Protection Agency to US Immigration and Customs Enforcement, and countless more.

The 2022 US Supreme Court decision rejecting the constitutionality of Biden administration actions—having failed to gain a majority in Congress to legislate its "climate change" proposals—to instead *impose* these policies through the EPA, was a setback to rule through fiat by bureaucracies. It was a setback, however temporary, to the tendency toward Bonapartism in the imperialist epoch.

The proletarian party's unconditional defense of the constitutional freedom of worship is indivisible from its defense of freedom of speech and assembly.

The Supreme Court in recent years has handed down decisions limiting government encroachments on other constitutional freedoms, as well. Several rulings have upheld the First Amendment right to "free exercise" of religion. These include court opinions permitting a high school coach to pray on the field at the end of a game; barring a state government from excluding religiously affiliated schools from access to public funding available to similar private schools with no religious connection; and reversing discriminatory government restrictions on holding religious services because of COVID quarantines.

The proletarian party's unconditional defense of the constitutional freedom of worship is indivisible from its defense of freedom of speech and assembly.

In recent years, Supreme Court Justice Elena Kagan has helped popularize among the self-designated enlightened the term "weaponizing the First Amendment." By this catchphrase, increasingly invoked by "progressives" and the "left," Kagan and others mean the alleged abuse of the Constitution's protection of freedom of speech and the press to air what the meritocracy considers "unacceptable" views, whether by opponents of abortion clinics, foes of so-called Critical Race Theory, advocates for the freedom to worship, or others.

At the same time, anti-working-class race-baiting, wokery, and "cancel culture" on the bourgeois and petty bourgeois left are fueling a rise of de facto book banning, the cancelation or disruption of speaking events and political debates, firings, and more. Both on the bourgeois left and right, school authorities and library boards are stripping books from shelves and classrooms—from Art Spiegelman's *Maus* to Harper Lee's *To Kill a Mockingbird*, from Anne Frank's *The Diary of a Young Girl* to Toni Morrison's *Beloved*. State and federal prison officials have been following suit.

9) The US Constitution is a bourgeois document, the supreme law of the land enshrining in writing the class dictatorship and property relations of what is today the world's final empire. When first drafted in the 1780s, as a product of the victory of the First American Revolution, the Constitution balanced the factional interests of Northern merchant capital and the plantation-based capital of the Southern slavocracy. By the mid-1800s that shaky ruling-class coalition erupted into the "inevitable conflict," the battle over secession. The resulting bloody civil war was the final manifestation of the mounting threat posed by the expansion of chattel slavery to the continent-wide consolidation of US commercial, banking, and industrial capital.

Also from the day the Constitution was ratified on June 21, 1788, there were struggles by small farmers, craftsmen, mechanics, and other plebeian layers, former slaves and bonded laborers, and later the rapidly expanding hereditary proletariat and other exploited producers to protect their class interests within this new governmental structure. Through hard-fought battles, they won amendments— *changes*—to the Constitution that provide protections *from* the state and exploiting class on whose behalf it rules.

Protections of the US Constitution limiting the reach of the bourgeois state are deeply in the interests of workers and our allies among working farmers and other exploited producers.

These rights, in addition to others widely established well before the first American Revolution, introduce a degree of rule by law and written boundaries on the rulers' license to run roughshod over popular and regional interests, rural as well as urban, and other expressions of social, cultural, religious, race, and national diversity among the toiling majority of a vast continent.

There is not a "Constitution," plus a separate Bill of Rights and other amendments. The twenty-seven current amendments *are part of* the US Constitution. These include the Thirteenth, Fourteenth, and Fifteenth Amendments, often called "the Reconstruction Amendments," which are conquests of the Second American Revolution.

Due to these historical origins and class battles, the US Constitution includes universal rights limiting the reach of the bourgeois state, protections that are deeply in the interests of workers and our allies among working farmers, owner-operator truckers, fishermen, small proprietors, and other exploited producers.

Standing guard against assaults on freedoms guaranteed by the Constitution is indispensable to engaging in the revolutionary class struggle necessary to prepare a vanguard of the working class capable, as conditions demand, of initiating and leading workers defense guards in the unions. Defense guards that can take on and defeat rightist and fascist forces that will organize at the service of the employing class with the aim of crushing the labor movement and its allies in face of a proletarian challenge to the rule of capital.

This course is central to the communist program, continuity, and practice of the Socialist Workers Party, along the line of march toward a revolutionary struggle for workers power.

II.

Capitalism's erosion of the family and the working-class road to women's emancipation

10) The economic, social, and moral crises of US and world capitalism undermine prospects for young people to begin families and provide for them. This is true especially for working-class youth. A growing percentage live with parents well into adulthood, and remain substantially dependent on them economically. The birth rate in the United States has declined for more than seventy years, reaching its lowest level ever. It has fallen to roughly 11 births per 1,000 people today from more than 24 in 1950, the high point of the mirage of "our" victory in World War II.

Working people in cities, small towns, and rural areas continue to face the scourge of opioids and other deadly drugs, including drug combinations laced with fentanyl. Gambling is massively promoted by the capitalist rulers in newspaper sports pages, over television, and through on-line "sportsbooks," leading to an accelerating rise in addiction. Alcoholism, mental illness, suicide, domestic violence, and crime are on the rise.

Paying for food, gasoline, housing, medical care, child-care, and other necessities is increasingly difficult for the families of workers, farmers, and other exploited producers. Steady employment at wages sufficient to sustain a family is less and less available.

Today's class reality emphatically confirms the statement in the 1938 founding program of the SWP and our world movement, drafted by Leon Trotsky, that unemployment and rising prices remain the "two basic economic afflictions, in which is summarized the increasing absurdity of the capitalist system."

These conditions, increasingly inflicted on working people of all national origins and skin colors, corroborate the conclusion drawn by Daniel Patrick Moynihan in his 1965 government report, *The Negro Family.* The disintegration over decades of families among working people who are Black, he noted, was a major factor underlying tens of millions of young African Americans "falling further and further behind," as measured by levels of employment, poverty, health, education, drug addiction, and crime.

Far from being an "African American affliction," nearly six decades later this family breakdown has spread much more broadly throughout the working class, as well as among other small producers and proprietors.

To cite a stunning example, the percentage of children in the United States growing up in homes with only one parent, usually a mother, has nearly tripled since Moynihan's *The Negro Family* was written. It has jumped from 9 percent in 1960 to 25 percent today. For children who are African American, the figure has jumped from around 20 percent in the 1960s to more than half today.

The economic and social consequences for working people of all skin colors and both sexes are heavy. Under capitalism the family is what children, the jobless, the elderly, the sick and disabled have to fall back on.

11) Central to any communist program is a union-led fight for *employment*, with wage rates, work schedules, and job conditions necessary for families to live, rather than be torn apart by the bosses' relentless drive for profits. As our 1938 program affirms, "*The right to employment* is the only serious right left to the worker in a society based upon exploitation." And thus our starting point.

Jobs, not dependence on welfare programs, open a road forward. The historical record shows that after every substantial cyclical crisis of capitalism, the families of working people on welfare are poorer than they had been coming out of the prior downturn. Working people need a course that strengthens confidence in our own worth and our ability to organize together and fight. A course that helps the working class and unions forge alliances with farmers, other exploited producers, and the oppressed.

Class-conscious workers call for a shorter workweek with no cut in pay, with regular hours. We call for a massive public works program to provide employment for millions at union-scale wages building hospitals, schools, childcare centers, housing, bridges, roads, and other needed infrastructure. In face of inflation, we demand cost-of-living escalators for wages (as well as retirement, jobless, and disability payments).

These are among the central demands a class-struggle left wing of the labor movement would organize the unions to lead the working class in fighting for.

As the working class and unions carry out these class battles, millions of families need to supplement their incomes.

Not by trying to hold down two or three jobs, leaving no time to relax and to think, no time for union, political, and social activity, no time for families.

Not by dependence on "means-tested" welfare programs and government "poverty" bureaucracies that shame and stigmatize recipients, that create conditions that block people from holding a job, and that tear families apart.

What is needed is a floor *for all families* of working people—an income that's sufficient for workers to maintain steady employment, as the labor movement fights for universal childcare and medical care. Enough to enable our class to maintain its solidarity, trade union activity, and the vanguard élan necessary for struggle.

In 1970, by a nearly two-to-one bipartisan majority, a bill establishing a Family Assistance Plan was adopted in the Democratic Party–controlled House of Representatives. The legislation had been introduced by the Republican Nixon administration; Moynihan had a substantial hand in drafting and promoting it. But the Democratic Party led the bill to defeat in the Senate, with liberals overwhelmingly voting no, supported by top trade union officials and leaders of the National Welfare Rights Organization. Many in the Senate's Republican minority trailed behind.

Liberal Democrats, in fact, kept pushing the "welfare is better" line, rather than a guaranteed income supplement for families, a program that encouraged employment rather than dependence on welfare payments.

Then, in the 1990s, liberals virtually all fell in step behind the Clinton administration in dumping Aid to Families with Dependent Children altogether. The Democrats had no plan of any sort to provide jobs, food, or housing for the millions who had been receiving such payments, especially single mothers and their children. As explained by SWP national secretary Jack Barnes in *The Clintons' Anti-Working-Class Record,* by then it was Senator Moynihan who, along with only a handful of other Democrats, voted against this reactionary legislation. Moynihan, in a letter to the White House, wrote that Clinton's "welfare reform" was "the most brutal act of social policy since Reconstruction" (or more precisely, since *the bloody defeat* of Reconstruction).

These are important political and programmatic questions to talk about in our unions, with coworkers on the job, and with workers engaged in strikes and other struggles over wages and conditions, as we organize solidarity and strengthen the labor movement.

We also discuss these issues with workers and all the exploited and oppressed as we campaign for SWP candidates, expand the weekly readership of the *Militant,* and introduce books that offer a revolutionary road forward for working people.

12) As a central part of this program, we fight for women's right to reproductive and maternal health care, sex education (not gender indoctrination), as well as access to the safest and most reliable contraceptive methods and safe and legal abortion procedures.

This is the opposite of the course of bourgeois and middle-class "population bomb" crusaders, whose alarms about the "overly fecund" races and "feeble-minded" social classes served as the pretext for more than sixty thousand *officially recorded* forced sterilizations of women in the United States from 1907 to 1981. Plus many thousands more in the US colony of Puerto Rico, where the island's Department of Health reported in the mid-1960s that some 35 percent of women of child-bearing age at that time had been sterilized—35 percent!

Despite the disavowal by Planned Parenthood of its initial "eugenic" views and those of its founder, Margaret Sanger, in the early twentieth century, anti-working-class "overpopulation" demagogy is still rife among bourgeois and middle-class "environmentalists," climate doomsayers, scientists, and organizations claiming to champion women's rights. This includes "counseling" working-class women and their spouses, often misrepresented as family planning, to bring fewer children into the world.

There can be no road to either Black liberation or women's emancipation separate and apart from the working-class struggle to confront capitalism's social crises bearing down on working people and their families. That, in turn, requires a class-struggle course to address the challenges and responsibilities that fall overwhelmingly on women as the bearers and nurturers of new life.

13) Within this communist course of conduct, SWP members can explain to fellow workers and champions of women's emancipation why the Supreme Court's reversal of *Roe v. Wade* in June 2022 is positive and valuable for our fight. It has opened the door to a broader and necessary debate to win a majority of the working class in each of the fifty states and US "territories" to support decriminalization. And to win them to understanding why, without access to legal and medically safe abortion, women—who have been oppressed as a sex since the emergence of class-divided society millennia ago—will always remain "the second sex" under capitalist social relations.

Supporters of women's equality can and must do what bourgeois and petty bourgeois leaderships have refused to do for five decades—wage a *political* fight among working people to reclaim the banner of "life" from anti-working-class, anti-woman forces, whose political objectives have nothing to do with the well-being of our families, including children, the elderly, and the infirm.

The party that fights for the liberation of the working class and all humanity is the party of life. That's who members of the Socialist Workers Party, and cadres of the communist movement worldwide, are.

14) The 1973 *Roe v. Wade* decision was an unvarnished example of the anti-constitutional exertion of "raw judicial power," as dissenting Justice Byron White, a Kennedy administration appointee, frankly put it at the time. At a single stroke, and without any constitutional foundation, the decision imposed a hotly disputed policy—with deep social and moral implications involving human life—on all human beings across fifty states, the District of Columbia, and US possessions and colonies.

In doing so, the "liberal" court short-circuited the nationwide debate on women's rights, in which supporters of emancipation had just begun to make some headway. Between 1967 and 1973, four US states had repealed laws criminalizing abortion—Hawaii, Alaska, New York, and Washington—and thirteen had expanded medical exceptions and exemptions for rape or incest.

The June 2022 Supreme Court decision *Dobbs v. Jackson Women's Health Organization* overruled *Roe's* anti-constitutional judicial diktat, stating: "The Constitution does not prohibit the citizens of each state from regulating or prohibiting abortion. *Roe* and *Casey* [a 1992 Supreme Court decision that, per *Dobbs*, "reaffirmed Roe's central holding, but pointedly refrained from endorsing most of its reasoning"] arrogated that authority.... We now return that authority to the people and their elected representatives."

As Justice Brett Kavanaugh wrote in his concurring opinion, the issue in the *Dobbs* case was "not the policy or morality of abortion.... The Constitution does not take sides on the issue of abortion. The text of the Constitution does not refer to or encompass abortion.... On the question of abortion, the Constitution is therefore neither pro-life nor pro-choice. The Constitution is neutral and leaves the issue for the people and their elected representatives to resolve through the democratic process in the States or Congress— like the numerous other difficult questions of American social and economic policy that the Constitution does not address. Because the Constitution is neutral on the issue of abortion, this Court also must be scrupulously neutral."

Protection against laws and punishments being dictated by the judiciary—a small, unelected branch of the capitalist state—is a constitutional safeguard to be prized and defended by working people and the oppressed.

Communist workers must answer the widely peddled falsehood that the Supreme Court's *Dobbs* decision struck down a woman's right to choose abortion. Such feverish claims have been purposely cranked up by liberals and the "left" in an effort to maximize Democratic Party electoral gains and at least minimize losses in the 2022 and 2024 state and federal elections.

In fact, *Dobbs* neither bars nor restricts abortions in a single state, including Mississippi. In the wake of *Dobbs*, such procedures and medications remain legal by state decision in more than twenty states, including some of the largest in population, such as New York and California. Some state legislatures have moved to further restrict or to bar

There's no road to Black freedom or women's emancipation separate from the working-class struggle to confront capitalism's social crises bearing down on working people and their families.

SUSAN LAMONT/MILITANT

Top: Brookwood, Alabama, August 2021. Members of International Longshoremen's Association from three states join rally for miners on strike against Warrior Met Coal.

Middle: Sacramento, February 2020. Childcare providers in California turn in 10,000 signatures in fight for union recognition.

SERVICE EMPLOYEES INTERNATIONAL UNION LOCAL 99

Bottom: London, December 2022. Nurses picket hospital as part of work stoppages across the United Kingdom. They demanded improved job conditions and wage raise to keep up with inflation.

KIRSTY WIGGLESWORTH/AP

abortions. In Kansas, however, a referendum aimed at facilitating an abortion ban went down to defeat by a 59–41 percent margin with a large voter turnout, and in November 2022 two other such referenda were defeated in Kentucky and Montana.

The Socialist Workers Party unconditionally supports decriminalization of abortion and joins others in fighting for it.

Contrary to defenders of *Roe v. Wade*—from the three Supreme Court justices dissenting from *Dobbs*; to President Biden and former Democratic presidents Obama, Clinton, and Carter; to liberal and radical voices of many stripes—the recent court ruling does not open a "slippery slope" undermining constitutional protections won by working people and the oppressed since the 1950s.

To the contrary. The *Dobbs* decision does not threaten "Miranda" warning protections for the accused. It does not jeopardize access to and use of various methods of contraception, privacy of sexual relations between consenting adults, or legalization of marriage between individuals of the same sex. Much less does it endanger the 1967 ruling that struck down reactionary state laws against "race-mixing" marriage between African Americans and Caucasians. The Supreme Court decision states unequivocally that it "does not undermine [these rights] in any way."

15) The Socialist Workers Party unconditionally supports the decriminalization of abortion and joins others in fighting for it. We do so for the reasons the communist

movement has always stood for this position, from Lenin and the Bolsheviks to this day.

Our position flows from our support for the emancipation of women, half of humankind, from all forms of oppression imposed during millennia of class society. This includes freedom from all political obstacles to full and equal participation in social and economic life and activity, as well as a woman's right to decide matters related to her own life and health, free of veto by husbands, brothers, uncles, other family members, courts, or legislatures.

At the same time, our communist program has nothing in common with bourgeois and middle-class forces—whether feminists, or campaigners for population control—who in fact advocate abortion as a means of contraception. We reject the pseudoscientific views of those who deny that the issue of human life, a profound moral question for all working people, is always involved in abortion decisions and procedures.

16) These communist positions are in continuity with those of V.I. Lenin, presented in his article "The Working Class and Neo-Malthusianism," published in 1913 in the Bolshevik newspaper *Pravda*.

Underlining the inhumane and anti-working-class realities of capitalist society, Lenin—using words that left no doubt as to his views—pointed to "the exceedingly widespread practice of destroying the fetus in present-day so-called civilized states," including tsarist Russia.

The Bolshevik leader recoiled at speeches made during a bourgeois medical conference in Russia that year advocating propaganda and counseling of working-class and lower-middle-class women to bring fewer children into the world. (Today such advice might well be heard at a "progressive" environmental gathering.) He rejected the "whisper" of those in the petty bourgeoisie, frightened by the "torments and hard toil" of capitalist conditions: "God grant we manage somehow by ourselves. So much the better if we have no children."

Lenin contrasted the reactionary ugliness of "population control" to the outlook of class-conscious workers, who say: "We're laying the foundation of a new edifice. Our children will complete its construction."

Condemning such "neo-Malthusian" fears and practices, Lenin contrasted "the completely reactionary nature and ugliness" of such an outlook to that of "the class-conscious worker," who is confident in "the working-class movement and its aims" and who says instead: "We are already laying the foundation of a new edifice and our children will complete its construction"—and their children, and their children!

SWP leader Joseph Hansen's 1960 *Militant* series, published later as the pamphlet *Too Many Babies? The Myth of the Population Explosion*, stands well alongside Lenin's 1913 article. Hansen popularizes the explanations by Karl Marx and Frederick Engels rebutting the reactionary views of Parson Thomas Malthus, the great grandfather of all population-control hucksters from the eighteenth century to the present day.

Half a decade after his polemic against neo-Malthusianism, Lenin called the toilers of the tsarist prison house of nations to insurrection. Under Bolshevik leadership, they conquered state power from the capitalists and landlords in Russia and began forging a voluntary federation of workers and peasants republics. A *voluntary* federation.

As the new proletarian dictatorship turned its program into deeds the birth rate—having fallen steeply during World War I and the death throes of the old regime—increased sharply in the young Soviet Union. It did so for more than a decade, despite the bloody civil war unleashed by the expropriated exploiters and accompanying imperialist invasions. By the opening of 1930s, this revolutionary enthusiasm among working people to bring new lives into the world had begun to be throttled by the Stalinist counterrevolution.

"It goes without saying," Lenin concluded in the 1913 article, that uncompromising opposition to population control "does not by any means prevent us from demanding the unconditional annulment of all laws against abortions or against the distribution of medical literature on contraceptive measures, etc. Such laws are nothing but the hypocrisy of the ruling classes. These laws do not heal the ulcers of capitalism; they merely turn them into malignant ulcers that are especially painful for the oppressed masses."

After the Bolshevik Revolution, this proletarian position was codified by the "Decree on Women's Health" of the Soviet workers and peasants republic. In November 1920 it became the first government in the world to decriminalize abortion. It did so as *an indispensable part* of advancing the social equality and health of women and ameliorating conditions for the working class and peasantry. The 1920 decree was signed by Nikolai Semashko and Dmitri

Kurskii, people's commissars of health and of justice in the Soviet republic.

"During the past decades, the number of women resorting to artificial termination of pregnancy has grown both in the West and in this country," the decree opened. "The legislation of all countries combats this evil by punishing the woman who chooses to have an abortion and the doctor who performs it. Without leading to favorable results, this [wrong] method of combating abortions has driven the operation underground and made the woman a victim of mercenary and ignorant quacks who make a profession of these secret operations. . . .

"The Workers' and Peasants' Government is conscious of this serious evil to the community. It combats this evil by propaganda against abortions among working women. By working for socialism, and by introducing the protection of Maternal and Child Welfare on an extensive scale, it feels assured of achieving the gradual disappearance of this evil.

"But as the moral survivals of the past and the difficult economic conditions of the present still compel many women to resort to this operation, the People's Commissariats of Health and of Justice, concerned to protect the health of women and considering that the method of repressions in this field fails entirely to achieve this aim, have decided . . . to permit such operations to be done freely and without any charge in Soviet hospitals, where conditions are assured of minimizing the harm of the operation."

17) Through their class-collaborationist orientation, including political subordination to the imperialist parties (largely to the Democratic Party since the second half of the 1930s), both the trade union officialdom and leaderships of organizations claiming to speak on behalf of women

share the major responsibility for setbacks to the struggle for women's equality. They rejected the only political course that could have stemmed the five-decade-long decline of access to abortion under medically safe conditions, especially for women in the working class and in rural areas, including Native American lands.

Frederick Engels, the founder of modern communism together with Karl Marx, pointed the way forward in 1885, when he wrote: "True equality between men and women can become a reality only when the exploitation of both by capital has been abolished, and private work in the home has been transformed into a public industry."

The revolutionary Soviet republic under the leadership of Lenin and the Bolsheviks, and some decades later the Cuban socialist revolution under the leadership of Fidel Castro, created the first opportunities in history for a government of the working class to organize and lead a fight for women's emancipation.

The domestic slavery confronting women, Lenin said, will change "only where and when an all-out struggle begins (led by the proletariat wielding the state power) against this petty housekeeping, or rather when its *wholesale transformation* into a large-scale socialist economy begins."

Only the proletarian dictatorship could begin—begin!—eliminating the economic compulsion on which the oppression of women in all class-divided societies has been founded.

In both the USSR and in Cuba that revolutionary course began with electrification, including in the most isolated regions of the country, to advance all aspects of social, economic, and cultural transformation. It required eradicating illiteracy. It required providing apartments and rural dwellings with running water and sanitation, as well as schools, jobs, medical care, education in health and hygiene, laundries, and childcare centers. It required combating drunkenness, drug abuse, domestic violence, and gambling.

Lessons from these proletarian-led revolutions are central to our communist continuity and internationalism. These include lessons from the blows the Stalin-led counterrevolution in the USSR and Communist International dealt to women and their families from the latter 1920s to the collapse of that Stalinist regime in the closing years of the twentieth century.

A course to address the capitalist-caused crises bearing down on families in the working class and among other toilers is at the center of the fight for women's emancipation today.

It begins with the fight by the working class to create the material and social conditions that will enable women and men to realize the basic conditions of our humanity. That means full participation in social labor and the ability to make conscious decisions, benefiting from advances in science and technology, including medical science, related to both production and human reproduction.

The road to the emancipation of the working class is the road to eradicating the historical roots not only of women's second-class status, but all forms of exploitation, oppression, and extreme coarseness under capitalism, the final stage of class society and its brutalities.

III.

The Cuban socialist revolution and our communist continuity

18) The Cuban socialist revolution—under the leadership of Fidel Castro, seasoned Rebel Army combatants, and other Cuban fighters won to its proletarian internationalist course—did not simply transform the lives, conditions, and political consciousness of workers and farmers in Cuba. That revolution, like the Bolshevik Revolution before it, opened a renewal of communist leadership in the Americas, in the United States and beyond.

From the Castro-led assault on the Moncada barracks in Santiago de Cuba and Bayamo garrison on July 26, 1953— and publication the next year of *History Will Absolve Me*, Fidel's courtroom defense of the aims of the revolution— the revitalization of communism began, both in program and in action.

Cadres of the Socialist Workers Party, from our origins within the American section of the Communist International in 1919, have understood that proletarian internationalism and class solidarity are carried out, first and foremost, as we build a revolutionary working-class party to advance the socialist revolution in the countries where we live, work, and fight.

Building such a party, and leading along that course toward a victorious struggle for workers power in the US, is the permanent centerpiece of what working people in this country contribute to ending Washington's economic, trade, financial, and political war against the toilers of Cuba—a policy carried out by *every* Democratic and Republican administration since 1959.

Since 1959 Cuba's workers and farmers, their revolutionary government, and their political leadership have held US imperialism at bay. They continue to do so, despite the brutal intensification of the US rulers' efforts to destroy the revolution.

The imperialist rulers' aim is to crush the spirit of Cuba's working people, their socialist revolution, and the example of working-class leadership and revolutionary intransigence they set for toilers in the United States, across the Americas, and worldwide. The message the US propertied rulers are signaling to working people here and everywhere is unvarnished: "This is what will be done to you if you work and fight to emulate Cuba's socialist revolution."

19) Since 1959 Cuba's workers and farmers, their revolutionary government, and their political leadership have held US imperialism at bay. They continue to do so, despite the brutal intensification of the US rulers' unrelenting efforts to destroy the revolution. The cumulative toll exacted over more than six decades by this all-encompassing imperialist assault weighs heavily on Cuban working people. The commodification of production and exchange, as well

Cuba's socialist revolution didn't just transform the lives and political consciousness of workers and farmers in Cuba. It opened a renewal of communist leadership in the US, the Americas, and beyond.

Above: May Day rally in Havana, 2022, was massive outpouring of Cuba's working people in defense of their socialist revolution and their determination to resist and turn back Washington's attempt to crush them.

Below: Havana, May 1, 1980. From right: Fidel Castro, with Maurice Bishop and Daniel Ortega, leaders of workers and farmers governments in Grenada and Nicaragua. Revolutionary victories in those countries in 1979 strengthened Cuba's socialist revolution. Today, the greatest burden borne by Cuban toilers is the absence of a single other victorious socialist revolution since 1959.

as the sway of the law of value—and its reflection in the attitudes of human beings—continues to expand.

The greatest burden borne by the Cuban toilers and their government is the absence of any new victorious socialist revolution for more than sixty years. In the 1970s and 1980s working people in Cuba gained new strength from the internationalist mission in Angola, which dealt a death blow to apartheid and white minority rule across Southern Africa.

The greatest burden borne by Cuba's toilers and their government is the absence of any new victorious socialist revolution for more than sixty years.

The Cuban Revolution was politically revitalized by the revolutionary workers and farmers governments in Grenada, led by Maurice Bishop, and in Nicaragua, under the leadership of the Sandinista National Liberation Front—what Fidel Castro in the early 1980s pointed to as "three giants rising up to defend their right to independence, sovereignty, and justice, on the very threshold of imperialism." The popular revolution in Burkina Faso in the mid-1980s, led by Thomas Sankara, brought reinforcement from West Africa.

None of these struggles culminated in a lasting extension of the world socialist revolution, for reasons the SWP has explained. While their political conquests and lessons remain indispensable, today there is not a single revolutionary working-class government anywhere in the world aside from Cuba.

These international factors and their social consequences in Cuba inevitably widen class divisions and social inequalities, raising the stakes in promoting and maintaining proletarian political consciousness and solidarity. Though weakened, the foundations of a living and fighting socialist revolution still stand.

In 2022, however, there can be no simple replay many decades later of the course led by Fidel Castro during the Rectification process that opened in 1986. Interlinked with the victorious culmination of the internationalist mission in Angola, the "Rectification of Errors and Negative Tendencies" brought renewed confidence to the Cuban working class. That class strength was decisive in the ability of Cuban working people to surmount the deep economic crisis of the 1990s—what Cubans call "the Special Period"—following the abrupt collapse of trade and financial relations with Stalinist regimes in the Soviet Union and Eastern and Central Europe.

Washington's determined drive to crush Cuba's example has been exacerbated by economic pressures of the global capitalist crisis that weigh heavily on all oppressed nations—rising prices, higher interest rates, the growing tendency toward capitalist stagflation on a world scale. Despite Cuba's exemplary response to COVID, the economic and social costs of the international pandemic have been heavy.

All these pressures have been amplified by the consequences of Moscow's invasion of Ukraine. Cuba's dependence on essential trade and aid from the capitalist regimes in Russia and China has increased. The solidarity extended by a number of Latin American and Caribbean governments, Venezuela especially, has been one of the bright spots on the horizon during a difficult year.

The greater hardships of everyday life have been registered in the migration of more than 200,000 Cubans to the United States in 2022, nearly double the last big wave of 125,000 in 1980, often identified as the Mariel boatlift.

A new revolutionary triumph or rise of substantial class battles in other parts of the world can impel a new direction in Cuba, as it would with revolutionary-minded working people in the United States and elsewhere in the Americas, Europe, Africa, the Middle East, and the Pacific and Asia.

20) These intertwined economic, social, and political developments bearing down on the Cuban Revolution come as no political or programmatic surprise to the Socialist Workers Party.

We were born as a party in 1919 with the founding of the Communist Party in the United States, and the forging of the Lenin-led Communist International of affiliated national parties. When our founding leaders were expelled in 1928 by the increasingly Stalin-dominated Comintern and CP misleaders, the initial issues of the *Militant* serialized a document by Leon Trotsky in defense of Lenin's proletarian internationalist program and rejecting the Russian nationalist program submitted in 1928 by the Comintern leadership to its Sixth World Congress.

The first chapter of Trotsky's document, "The Draft Program of the Communist International: A Criticism of Fundamentals," was entitled: "The Program of the International Revolution or a Program of Socialism in One Country?" It opened with these words: "In our epoch, which is the epoch of imperialism, i.e., of *world* economy and *world* politics under the hegemony of finance capital, not a single communist party can establish its program by proceeding solely or mainly from conditions and tendencies of developments in its own country."

"Of course the final victory of socialism in one country is impossible," Lenin had said at the very opening of the Bolshevik revolution in January 1918, and many times over in the years that followed. "But something else *is* possible: a living example, a getting to work somewhere in one country—that is what will set fire to the toiling masses in all countries."

And it did.

Again in May 1919 Lenin wrote: "Even if the imperialists should overthrow the Bolshevik power tomorrow, we should not regret for one second that we took the power. And not one of the class-conscious workers...would regret it, or would doubt that our revolution had nevertheless conquered."

Driving home Lenin's repeated insistence that there can be no enduring socialist victory in a single country, Trotsky pointed out that even "a socialist Germany"—the most industrially developed country in continental Europe—could not withstand isolation in a capitalist world.

In 1926, two years after Lenin's death, the rapidly degenerating leadership of the Communist International decreed that denial of "the possibility of the Soviet Union's maintaining itself for an indefinite length of time in a capitalist environment" was henceforth incompatible with Bolshevism. Socialism in one country was now Stalinist dogma, enforced on pain of expulsion, exile, imprisonment, or worse.

21) Given our Bolshevik continuity, no party is better prepared politically and programmatically, nor bears a greater responsibility, than the Socialist Workers Party and our co-thinkers in Canada, Europe, and the Pacific and Asia, to un-

derstand and explain the pressures bearing down on Cuba today. More important, no party is better prepared to keep on doing in 2022 what we pledged, in word and deed, to Cuban working people and their revolutionary leadership in the years after they stormed to victory in 1959.

That pledge was nothing new. It was what communist workers in the United States had been dedicating our lives and efforts to ever since 1919. We are building a working-class party *here* to organize and lead the working class and its allies in a revolutionary struggle for a workers and farmers government, opening the socialist revolution in the strongest bastion of world imperialism. We took history's "assignment" to emulate what Cuba's toilers had shown in life not only remains necessary but possible.

Whether in the pages of the *Militant,* or an SWP campaign speech, at a doorstep or on a picket line, or during the Havana International Book Fair and other activities in Cuba—what we say and what we do with regard to the Cuban Revolution does not begin by asking, *"How is Cuba doing?"* We instead ask and answer: *"How are we doing?"*

That above all is what revolutionary Cubans want to know. How well are we advancing as a proletarian party on our course to emulate the historic accomplishments of the Cuban toilers?

IV.

Forging a proletarian party
and educating its cadre

22) The SWP is forging a proletarian party in the United States—a revolutionary political instrument of the working class, whose purpose, as our constitution asserts in its opening clauses, is "to educate and organize the working class in order to establish a workers and farmers government, which will abolish capitalism in the United States and join in the worldwide struggle for socialism."

That task is inconceivable without placing at its center organizing the working class to build, extend, and strengthen trade unions and to use that union power to advance the interests of working people. A socialist revolution is impossible without the fight to transform the unions into instruments of class struggle, wielded by class-conscious, battle-tested workers.

We are part of trade union fights against the bosses, working through the unions as they are today. Our course is to be part of a growing component of the union movement engaged in resistance against the employers and their government. Only with that as our starting point, and advancing along that road, can SWP members take part in building a leadership able to organize a broad, fighting class-struggle left wing, one capable of transforming men and women as they transform the labor movement.

We are part of fights against the bosses, working through the trade unions as they are today.

A class-struggle left wing has yet to exist in the labor movement in the United States. Substantial progress toward building a class-struggle *leadership* of this kind was made in the 1930s by leaders of Minneapolis Teamsters Local 544 and of the Midwest over-the-road organizing drive.

23) The SWP is today concentrating our trade union-building efforts in the Bakery, Confectionery, Tobacco Workers, and Grain Millers International Union (BCTGM), and the freight rail unions in North America. We work together loyally with all union members as brothers and sisters—from our coworkers, to shop stewards and business agents, to union officials at local, district, and international levels.

Through our unions we help mobilize solidarity with strikes and other struggles, reaching out to the broad labor movement.

We are active in organizing efforts to bring workers who aren't yet union members, or who work in unorganized workplaces, into the union, thus building the union and strengthening the labor movement.

We make every effort to conduct ourselves as actively engaged, careful, knowledgeable, and competent trade union-

unionists. That's our job both as party members and members of our unions. That's our proletarian orientation and Marxist continuity, tested and confirmed in practice by the class-struggle leadership of the Teamsters battles in the 1930s and by our trade union work ever since, including during the turn to industry carried out by the party starting in the mid-1970s.

24) Consistent with this proletarian course in the unions, the party's activity to reach out with SWP campaigns to all exploited and oppressed toilers strengthens and extends the trade union work we're engaged in with working-class militants. As we gain the respect and confidence of co-workers and other union members, we also become better at effectively presenting our communist perspectives, including through the *Militant*, party election campaigns, and books that embody our program. And we recruit to the Socialist Workers Party.

In addition to our participation in gatherings and activities of the labor movement, we are alert to opportunities to bring our revolutionary class-struggle perspectives to those fighting for women's rights and Black liberation, as well as joining actions opposing Jew-hatred and anti-Semitic violence and activity against Washington's military intervention around the world and efforts to crush the Cuban Revolution.

25) The Socialist Workers Party is building and recruits to a proletarian cadre whose character, trustworthiness, norms, and habits of conduct—whose "way of life and activity," as succinctly put in the 1847 rules of the world's first communist organization—correspond with the party's aims and with its unconditional claim to loyalty and discipline from every member.

The norms of conduct set by Farrell Dobbs and others in the class-struggle leadership of the Midwest Teamsters battles, and by Malcolm X in his revolutionary political evolution during the final period of his life, are examples to learn from and emulate. There are no better resources helping us do so than Dobbs's four-volume Teamsters series and his two-volume *Revolutionary Continuity: Marxist Leadership in the U.S.*, as well as *Malcolm X, Black Liberation, and the Road to Workers Power* by SWP national secretary Jack Barnes.

The Socialist Workers Party is building a proletarian cadre whose character, trustworthiness, norms, and habits of conduct correspond with the party's political aims. That's the party we recruit to.

Drawing from the history of class struggles in the US and worldwide, Barnes underscores the programmatic lessons through which Malcolm "became the face and the authentic voice of the forces of the coming American revolution." Above all, the course presented in *Malcolm X, Black Liberation, and the Road to Workers Power*, Barnes notes, is a product of "the disciplined efforts" of Socialist Workers Party cadres—Black, Caucasian, and others—"who have been leading the work since the mid-1970s to build a party that is working class in composition as well as program and action," and "who, in their lives and activity, remain true to their revolutionary convictions to this day."

26) The cadre of a revolutionary working-class party must be educated in and politically internalize the Marx-

ist program, organizational principles, and history of the proletarian internationalist course of the SWP and world communist movement. That programmatic bedrock is presented in:

• "The Draft Program of the Communist International: A Criticism of Fundamentals," Trotsky's 1928 document cited earlier in this resolution, published in *The Third International after Lenin*. It is, as James P. Cannon said in his 1929 introduction, "a document of conflict written in the fires of the struggle to preserve [in the Communist International] the fundamental teachings of Marx and Lenin and maintain the proletarian dictatorship of the Soviet Union."

• *The Transitional Program*, the 1938 founding resolution of the Fourth International drafted by Trotsky in close collaboration with the Socialist Workers Party leadership. The world communist movement, our program says, "uncompromisingly gives battle to all political groupings tied to the apron-strings of the bourgeoisie. Its task—the abolition of capitalism's domination. Its aim—socialism. Its method—the proletarian revolution."

• *In Defense of Marxism*, the compilation of articles and letters by Trotsky to SWP leaders during the 1939–40 political struggle in the party against a petty bourgeois opposition bending to US imperialism's intensifying war drive. In it, Trotsky presents the Marxist theoretical, programmatic, and organizational reasons why, in his words, "The class composition of the party must correspond to its class program."

• The political importance of a parallel work, *The Struggle for a Proletarian Party* by James P. Cannon, was emphasized by Trotsky in an April 1940 letter to Farrell Dobbs. "Jim's pamphlet ... is the writing of a genuine workers leader,"

Trotsky wrote. If the political struggle against the petty bourgeois opposition in the party "had not produced more than this document, it would be justified."

• *Their Trotsky and Ours* by Jack Barnes, based on a December 1982 talk presented to a public meeting of one thousand in Chicago as part of a socialist educational conference held in conjunction with the Young Socialist Alliance national convention. The talk was given during the opening years of the turn to industry, Barnes later wrote, when "the Socialist Workers Party was becoming more proletarian in composition—in daily life—as well as in program."

Those were years, Barnes wrote, when "the unfolding revolutions in Central America and the Caribbean were underlining for us once again how, with working-class leadership, the toilers can use a workers and farmers government to advance toward the expropriation of the exploiters and oppressors, the establishment of the dictatorship of the proletariat." Years when "we could see and understand more richly and act with greater confidence on the continuity of our program and strategy" going back to Marx and Engels and the conquests of the Communist International under the leadership of Lenin and the Bolsheviks.

Grounded in these programmatic foundations, every party cadre can more deeply and more concretely internalize and act on the resolution adopted by our 1965 convention, *The Organizational Character of the Socialist Workers Party*. "The party strives for political homogeneity in the sense that admission to its ranks requires fundamental agreement with its program and principles," the resolution states. "For similar reasons unconditional loyalty and disciplined conduct are required as a condition of membership."

27) Our experiences in the United States since the last party convention confirm that the low point of working-class and labor resistance is behind us. There are more than ample opportunities to continue organizing and acting on our communist course, helping to build the nucleus of a class-struggle left-wing leadership in the unions, and recruiting to the Socialist Workers Party.

INDEX

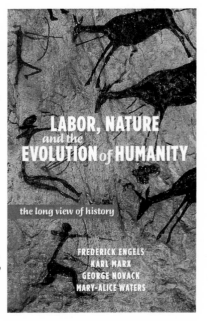

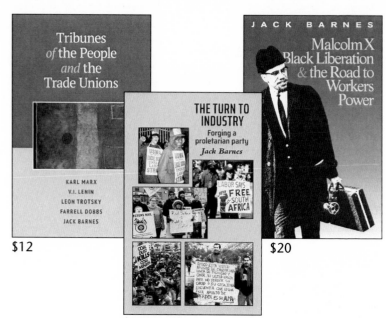

WOMEN'S EMANCIPATION AND THE WORKING CLASS

Women in Cuba: The Making of a Revolution within the Revolution

VILMA ESPÍN,
ASELA DE LOS SANTOS,
YOLANDA FERRER

The integration of women in the ranks and leadership of the Cuban Revolution was intertwined with the proletarian course of the leadership of the revolution from the start. This is the story of that revolution and how it transformed the women and men who made it. $17. Also in Spanish, Farsi, and Greek.

The Emancipation of Women

V.I. LENIN

The road to women's emancipation, Lenin wrote, begins "only when an all-out struggle begins, led by the proletariat wielding state power," to draw women as equals into productive social labor. And to begin transforming cooking, childcare, and other housework into social tasks of "a large-scale socialist economy." $7

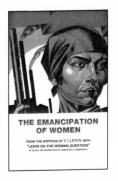

Cosmetics, Fashions, and the Exploitation of Women

JOSEPH HANSEN, EVELYN REED, MARY-ALICE WATERS

How big business reinforces women's second-class status and uses it to rake in profits. Where does women's oppression come from? How has the entry of millions of women into the workforce strengthened the battle for emancipation, still to be won? $12. Also in Spanish, Farsi, and Greek.

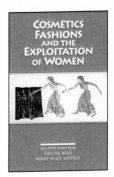

THE WORKING-CLASS STRUGGLE AND DEFENSE OF CONSTITUTIONAL FREEDOMS

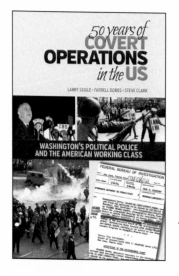

50 Years of Covert Operations in the US

Washington's Political Police and the American Working Class

LARRY SEIGLE, FARRELL DOBBS, STEVE CLARK

How class-conscious workers have fought against the drive to build the "national security" state essential to maintaining capitalist rule. $10. Also in Spanish and Farsi.

Socialism on Trial

Testimony at Minneapolis Sedition Trial

JAMES P. CANNON

The revolutionary program of the working class, presented in response to frame-up charges of "seditious conspiracy" in 1941, on the eve of US entry into World War II. The defendants were leaders of the Minneapolis labor movement and the Socialist Workers Party. $15. Also in Spanish, French, and Farsi.

FBI on Trial

The Victory in the Socialist Workers Party Suit against Government Spying

MARGARET JAYKO

The record of an historic victory in the fight for political rights, including the 1986 federal court ruling against government spying and excerpts from trial testimony by SWP leaders Farrell Dobbs and Jack Barnes. $17

The Teamster Series

FARRELL DOBBS

Four books on the strikes, organizing drives, and political campaigns that transformed the Teamsters across the Midwest in the 1930s into a militant industrial union movement.

How the class-struggle Teamsters leadership fought Washington's frame-up and imprisonment of leaders of Local 544 and the Socialist Workers Party, who were organizing to educate and mobilize class-conscious labor militants and the unions against US imperialist war aims in World War II.

A tool for workers seeking to use union power in every workplace and advance the fight for an independent labor party. $16 each, series $50. Also in Spanish. *Teamster Rebellion* is also available in French, Farsi, and Greek.

In Defense of Marxism

Against the Petty-Bourgeois Opposition in the Socialist Workers Party

LEON TROTSKY

A reply to those in the revolutionary workers movement in the late 1930s bending to bourgeois patriotism during Washington's buildup to enter World War II. Trotsky explains why only a party fighting to bring workers into its ranks and leadership can steer a communist course. In the process, he defends the materialist and dialectical foundations of Marxism. $17. Also in Spanish.

Cointelpro

The FBI's Secret War on Political Freedom

NELSON BLACKSTOCK

An in-depth look at the 1960s and '70s covert FBI disruption and counterintelligence program—code-named COINTELPRO. Contains reproductions of FBI documents released through the Socialist Workers Party suit against government spying. $15

COMMUNIST CONTINUITY
AND PROGRAM

The Transitional Program for Socialist Revolution

LEON TROTSKY

The Socialist Workers Party program, drafted by Trotsky in 1938, still guides the SWP and communists the world over. The party "uncompromisingly gives battle to all political groupings tied to the apron strings of the bourgeoisie. Its task—the abolition of capitalism's domination. Its aim—socialism. Its method—the proletarian revolution." $17. Also in Farsi.

The Third International after Lenin

LEON TROTSKY

Leon Trotsky's 1928 defense of the Marxist course that had guided the Communist International in its early years. Writing in the heat of political battle, Trotsky addresses the key challenge facing working people today: building communist parties throughout the world capable of leading workers and farmers to take power. $20. Also in Farsi.

Revolutionary Continuity

Marxist Leadership in the United States

The Early Years, 1848–1917
Birth of the Communist Movement, 1918–1922

FARRELL DOBBS

"Successive generations of proletarian revolutionists have participated in the movements of the working class and its allies.... Marxists today owe them not only homage for their deeds. We also have a duty to learn what they did wrong as well as right so their errors are not repeated." —*Farrell Dobbs*. Two volumes, $17 each.

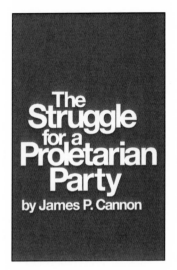

The Struggle for a Proletarian Party

JAMES P. CANNON

"The workers of America have power enough to topple the structure of capitalism at home and to lift the whole world with them when they rise," Cannon asserts. On the eve of World War II, a founder of the communist movement in the US and leader of the Communist International in Lenin's time defends the program and party-building norms of Bolshevism. $20. Also in Spanish and Farsi.

Their Trotsky and Ours

JACK BARNES

To lead the working class in a successful revolution, a mass proletarian party is needed whose cadres, well beforehand, have absorbed a world communist program, are proletarian in life and work, derive deep satisfaction from doing politics, and have forged a leadership with an acute sense of what to do next. This book is about building such a party. $12. Also in Spanish, French, and Farsi.

Organizational Character of the Socialist Workers Party

1965 Resolution of the SWP

Deepening capitalist crisis and sharpening class conflict demand a revolutionary solution. Active preparation for such struggles determines the kind of organization the Socialist Workers Party has set out to build from its birth. $5. Also in Spanish.

FROM PATHFINDER

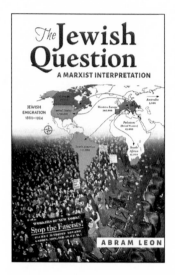

The Jewish Question

A Marxist Interpretation

ABRAM LEON

Why is Jew-hatred still raising its ugly head? What are its class roots—from antiquity through feudalism, to capitalism's rise and current crises? Why is there no solution under capitalism? The author, Abram Leon, was killed in the Nazi gas chambers. Revised translation, new introduction, and 40 pages of illustrations and maps. $17. Also in Spanish and French.

Opening Guns of World War III: Washington's Assault on Iraq

JACK BARNES

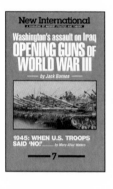

The murderous assault on Iraq in 1990–91 heralded increasingly sharp conflicts among imperialist powers, growing instability of capitalism, and more wars. Also includes:

1945: When US Troops Said No! by Mary-Alice Waters

Lessons from the Iran-Iraq War by Samad Sharif

In *New International* no. 7. $14. Also in Spanish, French, and Farsi.

U.S. Imperialism Has Lost the Cold War

JACK BARNES

The collapse of regimes across Eastern Europe and the USSR claiming to be communist did not mean workers and farmers there had been crushed. In today's sharpening capitalist conflicts and wars, these toilers are joining working people the world over in the class struggle against exploitation. In *New International* no. 11. $14. Also in Spanish, French, Farsi, and Greek.

The Clintons' Anti-Working-Class Record
Why Washington Fears Working People
JACK BARNES

What working people need to know about the profit-driven course of Democrats and Republicans alike over the last three decades. And the political awakening of workers seeking to understand and resist the capitalist rulers' assaults. $10. Also in Spanish, French, Farsi, and Greek.

Cuba and the Coming American Revolution
JACK BARNES

This is a book about the struggles of working people in the imperialist heartland, the youth attracted to them, and the example set by the Cuban people that revolution is not only necessary—it can be made. It is about the class struggle in the US, where the revolutionary capacities of workers and farmers are today as utterly discounted by the ruling powers as were those of the Cuban toilers. And just as wrongly. $10. Also in Spanish, French, and Farsi.

Are They Rich Because They're Smart?
Class, Privilege, and Learning under Capitalism
JACK BARNES

Exposes growing class inequalities in the US and the self-serving rationalizations of well-paid professionals who think their "brilliance" equips them to "regulate" working people, who don't know what's in our own best interest. $10. Also in Spanish, French, Farsi, and Arabic.

In Defense of the US Working Class

MARY-ALICE WATERS

Drawing on the fighting traditions of the oppressed and exploited of all colors and national origins, in 2018 tens of thousands of teachers and other working people in West Virginia, Oklahoma, and other states waged victorious strikes. They fought for dignity and respect for themselves, their families, and for all working people. $7. Also in Spanish, French, Farsi, and Greek.

America's Revolutionary Heritage

Marxist Essays

GEORGE NOVACK

A materialist explanation of the American Revolution, Civil War and Radical Reconstruction, genocide against the Indians, rise of American imperialism, first wave of the fight for women's rights, and more. $23

Labor's Giant Step

The First Twenty Years of the CIO: 1936–55

ART PREIS

The story of the explosive labor struggles and political battles in the 1930s that built the industrial unions. And how those unions became the vanguard of a mass social movement that began transforming US society. $27

Puerto Rico: Independence Is a Necessity

RAFAEL CANCEL MIRANDA

One of the five Puerto Rican Nationalists imprisoned by Washington for more than 25 years and released in 1979 speaks out on the brutal reality of US colonial domination, the example of Cuba's socialist revolution, and the ongoing struggle for independence. $5. Also in Spanish and Farsi.

Books for the Blind and Those with Low Vision

Pathfinder Press is making its titles, in English, as accessible ebooks. These are the first six.

What is an accessible ebook?

It is an electronic book (ebook) with these accessibility features:

Table of contents, notes, glossaries, and indexes have links that help readers find their way.

Page navigation is coded to correspond to the pages in the print book.

Short descriptions of each photograph, illustration, and chart in order to complement the print-book captions.

Who are they for?

Pathfinder ebooks are available to those with a reading or perceptual disability, a visual impairment, or a physical condition that affects their ability to read.

How to get Pathfinder ebooks?

They are available at www.bookshare.org. Visit the Bookshare website for information on how to sign up.

Ebooks can be downloaded in different file formats, including EPUB3, DAISY, and Braille Ready Format (BRF) files. Also available as audiobooks and through Bookshare's Reader.

W W W . P A T H F I N D E R P R E S S . C O M

REVOLUTIONARY LEADERS IN THEIR OWN WORDS

The Communist Manifesto

KARL MARX
AND FREDERICK ENGELS

Communism, say the founding leaders of the revolutionary workers movement, is not a set of ideas or preconceived "principles" but workers' line of march to power, springing from a "movement going on under our very eyes." $5. Also in Spanish, French, Farsi, and Arabic.

Thomas Sankara Speaks

The Burkina Faso Revolution, 1983–87

Under Sankara's guidance, Burkina Faso's revolutionary government led peasants, workers, women, and youth to expand literacy; to sink wells, plant trees, erect housing; to combat women's oppression; to carry out land reform; to join others worldwide to free themselves from the imperialist yoke. $20. Also in French.

Socialism: Utopian and Scientific

FREDERICK ENGELS

"To make men the masters of their own form of social organization—to make them free—is the mission of the modern proletariat," writes Engels. A classic guide to the operations of capitalism and struggles of the working class. $10. Also in Farsi.

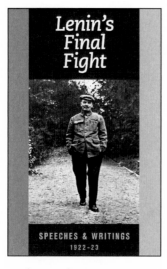

Lenin's Final Fight

Speeches and Writings, 1922–23

V.I. LENIN

In 1922 and 1923, V.I. Lenin, central leader of the world's first socialist revolution, waged what was to be his last political battle—one that was lost following his death. At stake was whether that revolution, and the international communist movement it led, would remain on the revolutionary proletarian course that brought workers and peasants to power in October 1917. $17. Also in Spanish, Farsi, and Greek.

Malcolm X Talks to Young People

"The young generation of whites, Blacks, browns, whatever else—you're living at a time of revolution," said Malcolm in 1964. "And I for one will join with anyone, I don't care what color you are, as long as you want to change this miserable condition that exists on this earth." Four talks and an interview in the last months of Malcolm's life. $12. Also in Spanish, French, Farsi, and Greek.

Socialism and Man in Cuba

ERNESTO CHE GUEVARA, FIDEL CASTRO

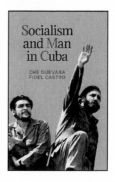

"Man truly reaches his full human condition when he produces without being compelled by physical necessity to sell himself as a commodity," wrote Guevara in 1965. $5. Also in Spanish, French, Farsi, and Greek.

PATHFINDER AROUND THE WORLD

UNITED STATES
(and Caribbean, Latin America, and East Asia)

Pathfinder Books, 306 W. 37th St., 13th Floor
New York, NY 10018

CANADA

Pathfinder Books, 7107 St. Denis, Suite 204
Montreal, QC H2S 2S5

UNITED KINGDOM
(and Europe, Africa, Middle East, and South Asia)

Pathfinder Books, 5 Norman Rd.
Seven Sisters, London N15 4ND

AUSTRALIA
(and New Zealand, Southeast Asia, and the Pacific)

Pathfinder Books, Suite 2, First floor, 275 George St.
Liverpool, Sydney, NSW 2170
Postal address: P.O. Box 73, Campsie, NSW 2194

JOIN THE PATHFINDER READERS CLUB
BUILD YOUR LIBRARY!

$10 / YEAR
25% DISCOUNT ON ALL PATHFINDER TITLES
30% OFF BOOKS OF THE MONTH
Valid at pathfinderpress.com and local Pathfinder book centers

Go to: www.pathfinderpress.com/
products/pathfinder-readers-club

Pathfinder
pathfinderpress.com